COMHAIRLE CHONTAE ÁTHA CLIATH THEAS

SOUTH DUBLIN COUNTY LIBRARIES

CASTLETYMON BRANCH LIBRARY

TO RENEW ANY ITEM   TEL. 452 4888

Items should be returned on or before the last date below. Fines, as displayed

in the Library, will be charged on overdue items.

15 JAN 98

22. MAR 02

DL →
due Te $\frac{10}{06}$ /02

03

22. OCT

THE GREAT HUNGER
Poem into Play

Essays and Texts in Cultural History II

THE GREAT HUNGER
Poem into Play

Patrick Kavanagh
&
Tom Mac Intyre

THE LILLIPUT PRESS
1988

First published in 1988 by
THE LILLIPUT PRESS LTD
Gigginstown, Mullingar,
Co. Westmeath, Ireland

British Library Cataloguing in Publication Data
Kavanagh, Patrick, 1904-1967
The great hunger: poem into play.
I. Title   II. Mac Intyre, Tom
821'.912

ISBN 0 946640 32 7

The poe[...] [...]anagh,
c[...]
[...]

Series editor: W. J. Mc Cormack

Cover design by Jarlath Hayes
Set in 10 on 12 Palatino by
Redsetter Ltd of Dublin
Printed by Billings & Sons Ltd of Worcester, England.

Contents

Editor's Preface

This contribution to the series follows a venerable example while also breaking new ground. The texts brought together here exist in a more complex relation than translation from one language to another. Tom Mac Intyre's stage transformation of Patrick Kavanagh's poem, *The Great Hunger*, should be read in an Irish cultural history of dramatized material made most memorable in Yeats's version of Cuchulain tales. Or, to borrow a phrase from from a different aspect of Yeats, here again we find that process of ancient renewal:

> *Those images that yet*
> *Fresh images beget*
> *That dolphin-torn, that gong-tormented sea.*

Mac Intyre may drastically distance himself from Yeats as a mentor, as a past-master, yet he pursues a similar objective in seeking to unite the old and the new. In *his Great Hunger* there arises a post-modernist splendour which the poem's author could hardly have anticipated. But whatever Yeats and Kavanagh might say about this new text, and its performance, Mac Intyre here takes up a central position in that he tackles a problem at the heart of our cultural inheritance – the absence of a truly popular theatre over the centuries. The vigour of his imagination is a measure of all that still needs to be supplied to make that inheritance replete, sufficient even.

Patrick Kavanagh
THE GREAT HUNGER

THE GREAT HUNGER

I

Clay is the word and clay is the flesh
Where the potato-gatherers like mechanised scare-crows move
Along the side-fall of the hill — Maguire and his men.
If we watch them an hour is there anything we can prove
Of life as it is broken-backed over the Book
Of Death? Here crows gabble over worms and frogs
And the gulls like old newspapers are blown clear of the hedges,
  luckily.
Is there some light of imagination in these wet clods?
Or why do we stand here shivering?
                              Which of these men
Loved the light and the queen
Too long virgin? Yesterday was summer. Who was it promised
  marriage to himself
Before apples were hung from the ceilings for Halloween?
We will wait and watch the tragedy to the last curtain
Till the last soul passively like a bag of wet clay
Rolls down the side of the hill, diverted by the angles
Where the plough missed or a spade stands, straitening the way.

A dog lying on a torn jacket under a heeled-up cart,
A horse nosing along the posied headland, trailing
A rusty plough. Three heads hanging between wide-apart
Legs. October playing a symphony on a slack wire paling.
Maguire watches the drills flattened out
And the flints of that lit candle for him on a June altar
Flameless. The drills slipped by and the days slipped by
And he trembled his head away and ran free from the world's
  halter,
And thought himself wiser than any man in the townland
When he laughed over pints of porter
Of how he came free from every net spread
In the gaps of experience. He shook a knowing head
And pretended to his soul

That children are tedious in hurrying fields of April
Where men are spanging across wide furrows.
Lost in the passion that never needs a wife—
The pricks that pricked were the pointed pins of harrows.
Children scream so loud that the crows could bring
The seed of an acre away with crow-rude jeers.
Patrick Maguire, he called his dog and he flung a stone in the air
And hallooed the birds away that were the birds of the years.

Turn over the weedy clods and tease out the tangled skeins.
What is he looking for there?
He thinks it is a potato, but we know better
Than his mud-gloved fingers probe in this insensitive hair.

"Move forward the basket and balance it steady
In this hollow. Pull down the shafts of that cart, Joe,
And straddle the horse" Maguire calls.
"The wind's over Brannagan's now that means rain.
Graip up some withered stalks and see that no potato falls
Over the tail-board going down the ruckety pass—
And *that's* a job we'll have to do in December,
Gravel it and build a kerb on the bog-side. Is that Cassidy's ass
Out in my clover? Curse o' God—
Where is that dog?
Never where he's wanted." Maguire grunts and spits
Through a clay-wattled moustache and stares about him from
   the height.
His dream changes again like the cloud-swung wind
And he is not so sure now if his mother was right
When she praised the man who made a field his bride.

Watch him, watch him, that man on a hill whose spirit
Is a wet sack flapping about the knees of time.
He lives that his little fields may stay fertile when his own body
Is spread in the bottom of a ditch under two coulters crossed in
   Christ's Name.

He was suspicious in his youth as a rat near strange bread.
When girls laughed; when they screamed he knew that meant
The cry of fillies in season. He could not walk

4

The easy road to his destiny. He dreamt
The innocence of young brambles to hooked treachery.
O the grip, O the grip of irregular fields! No man escapes.
It could not be that back of the hills love was free
And ditches straight.
No monster hand lifted up children and put down apes
As here.
                              "O God if I had been wiser!"
That was his sigh like the brown breeze in the thistles.
He looks towards his house and haggard. "O God if I had been
     wiser!"
But now a crumpled leaf from the whitethorn bushes
Darts like a frightened robin, and the fence
Shows the green of after-grass through a little window,
And he knows that his own heart is calling his mother a liar.
God's truth is life — even the grotesque shapes of its foulest fire.

The horse lifts its head and crashes
Through the whins and stones
To lip late passion in the crawling clover.
In the gap there's a bush weighted with boulders like morality
The fools of life bleed if they climb over.

The wind leans from Brady's, and the coltsfoot leaves are holed
     with rust,
Rain fills the cart-tracks and the sole-plate grooves;
A yellow sun reflects in Donaghmoyne
The poignant light in puddles shaped by hooves.

Come with me, Imagination, into this iron house
And we will watch from the doorway the years run back,
And we will know what a peasant's left hand wrote on the page.
Be easy October. No cackle hen, horse neigh, tree-sough, duck
     quack.

II

Maguire was faithful to death:
He stayed with his mother till she died

5

At the age of ninety one.
She stayed too long,
Wife and mother in one.
When she died
The knuckle-bones were cutting the skin of her son's backside
And he was sixty five.

O he loved his mother
Above all others.
O he loved his ploughs
And he loved his cows
And his happiest dream
Was to clean his arse
With perennial grass
On the bank of some summer stream;
To smoke his pipe
In a sheltered gripe
In the middle of July —
His face in a mist
And two stones in his fist
And an impotent worm on his thigh.

But his passion became a plague
For he grew feeble bringing the vague
Women of his mind to lust nearness,
Once a week at least flesh must make an appearance.

So Maguire got tired
Of the no-target gun fired
And returned to his headlands of carrots and cabbage
To the fields once again
Where eunuchs can be men
And life is more lousy than savage.

III

Poor Paddy Maguire, a fourteen hour day
He worked for years. It was he that lit the fire
And boiled the kettle and gave the cows their hay.

His mother tall hard as a Protestant spire
Came down the stairs bare-foot at the kettle call
And talked to her son sharply: "Did you let
The hens out, you?" She had a venomous drawl
And a wizened face like moth-eaten leatherette.
Two black cats peeped between the banisters
And gloated over the bacon-fizzling pan
Outside the window showed tin canisters.
The snipe of Dawn fell like a whirring noise
And Patrick on a headland stood alone.

The pull is on the traces, it is March
And a cold old black wind is blowing from Dundalk.
The twisting sod rolls over on her back —
The virgin screams before the irresistible sock.
No worry on Maguire's mind this day
Except that he forgot to bring his matches.
"Hop back there Polly, hoy back, woa, wae"
From every second hill a neighbour watches
With all the sharpened interest of rivalry.
Yet sometimes when the sun comes through a gap
These men know God the Father in a tree:
The Holy Spirit is the rising sap,
And Christ will be the green leaves that will come
At Easter from the sealed and guarded tomb.

Primroses and the unearthly start of ferns
Among the blackthorn shadows in the ditch,
A dead sparrow and an old waistcoat. Maguire learns
As the horses turn slowly round the which is which
Of love and fear and things half born to mind.
He stands between the plough-handles and he sees
At the end of a long furrow his name signed
Among the poets, prostitute's. With all miseries
He is one. Here was the unfortunate
Who for half moments of paradise
Pay out good days and wait and wait
For sunlight-woven cloaks. O to be wise
As Respectability that knows the price of all things
And marks God's truth in pounds and pence and farthings.

7

IV

April, and no one able to calculate
How far it is to harvest. They put down
The seeds blindly with sensuous groping fingers,
And sensual sleep dreams subtly underground.
To-morrow is Wednesday — who cares?
"Remember Eileen Farrelly? I was thinking
A man might do a damned sight worse. . " That voice is blown
Through a hole in a garden wall —
And who was Eileen now cannot be known.

The cattle are out on grass,
The corn is coming up evenly.
The farm folk are hurrying to catch Mass:
Christ will meet them at the end of the world, the slow and
    speedier.
But the fields say: only Time can bless.

Maguire knelt beside a pillar where he could spit
Without being seen. He turned an old prayer round:
"Jesus, Mary and Joseph pray for us
Now and at the Hour." Heaven dazzled death.
"Wonder should I cross-plough that turnip-ground."
The tension broke. The congregation lifted its head
As one man and coughed in unison.
Five hundred hearts were hungry for life —
Who lives in Christ shall never die for the death.
And the candle-lit Altar and the flowers
And the pregnant Tabernacle lifted a moment to Prophecy
Out of the clayey hours.
Maguire sprinkled his face with holy water
As the congregation stood up for the Last Gospel.
He rubbed the dust off his knees with his palm, and then
Coughed the prayer phlegm up from his throat and sighed:
    Amen.

Once one day in June when he was walking
Among his cattle in the Yellow Meadow
He met a girl carrying a basket —

8

And he was then a young and heated fellow.
Too earnest, too earnest! He rushed beyond the thing
To the unreal. And he saw Sin
Written in letters larger than John Bunyan dreamt of.
For the strangled impulse there is no redemption.
And that girl was gone and he was counting
The dangers in the fields where love ranted
He was helpless. He saw his cattle
And stroked their flanks in lieu of wife to handle.
He would have changed the circle if he could,
The circle that was the grass track where he ran.
Twenty times a day he ran round the field
And still there was no winning post where the runner is cheered
    home.
Desperately he broke the tune,
But however he tried always the same melody crept up from the
    background
The dragging step of a ploughman going home through the
    guttery
Headlands under an April-watery moon.
Religion, the fields and the fear of the Lord
And Ignorance giving him the coward's blow
He dare not rise to pluck the fantasies
From the fruited Tree of Life. He bowed his head
And saw a wet weed twined about his toe.

V

Evening at the cross-roads —
Heavy heads nodding out words as wise
As the rumination of cows after milking.
From the ragged road surface a boy picks up
A piece of gravel and stares at it — and then
He flings it across the elm tree on to the railway.
It means nothing,
Not a damn thing.
Somebody is coming over the metal railway bridge.
And his hob-nailed boots on the arches sound like a gong
Calling men awake. But the bridge is too narrow —

The men lift their heads a moment. That was only John,
So they dream on.

Night in the elms, night in the grass.
O we are too tired to go home yet. Two cyclists pass
Talking loudly of Kitty and Molly —
Horses or women? wisdom or folly?

A door closes on an evicted dog
Where prayers begin in Barney Meegan's kitchen;
Rosie curses the cat between her devotions;
The daughter prays that she may have three wishes —
Health and wealth and love —
From the fairy who is faith or hope or compounds of.

At the cross-roads the crowd had thinned out:
Last words are uttered. There is no to-morrow;
No future but only time stretched for the mowing of the hay
Or putting an axle in the turf-barrow.

Patrick Maguire went home and made coco
And broke a chunk off the loaf of wheaten bread;
His mother called down to him to look again
And make sure that the hen-house was locked. His sister
    grunted in bed
The sound of a sow taking up a new position.
Pat opened his trousers wide over the ashes
And dreamt himself to lewd sleepiness
The clock ticked on. Time passes.

VI

Health and wealth and love he too dreamed of in May
As he sat on the railway slope and watched the children of the
    place
Picking up a primrose here and a daisy there —
They were picking up life's truth singly. But he dreamt
    of the Absolute envased bouquet —
All or nothing. And it was nothing. For God is not all

In one place, complete and labelled like a case in a railway store
Till Hope comes in and takes it on his shoulder —
O Christ, that is what you have done for us:
In a crumb of bread the whole mystery is.

He read the symbol too sharply and turned
From the five simple doors of sense
To the door whose combination lock has puzzled
Philosopher and priest and common dunce.

Men build their heavens as they build their circles
Of friends. God is in the bits and pieces of Everyday —
A kiss here and a laugh again, and sometimes tears,
A pearl necklace round the neck of poverty.

He sat on the railway slope and watched the evening,
Too beautifully perfect to use,
And his three wishes were three stones too sharp to sit on,
Too hard to carve. Three frozen idols of a speechless muse.

VII

"Now go to Mass and pray and confess your sins
And you'll have all the luck" his mother said.
He listened to the lie that is a woman's screen
Around a conscience when soft thighs are spread.
And all the while she was setting up the lie
She trusted in Nature that never deceives.
But her son took it as the literal truth.
Religion's walls expand to the push of nature. Morality yields
To sense — but not in little tillage fields.

Life went on like that. One summer morning
Again through a hay-field on her way to the shop —
The grass was wet and over-leaned the path —
And Agnes held her skirts sensationally up,
And not because the grass was wet either.
A man was watching her, Patrick Maguire.
She was in love with passion and its weakness

And the wet grass could never cool the fire
That radiated from her unwanted womb
In that country, in that metaphysical land
Where flesh was a thought more spiritual than music
Among the stars — out of the reach of the peasant's hand.

Ah, but the priest was one of the people too —
A farmer's son — and surely he knew
The needs of a brother and sister.
Religion could not be a counter-irritant like a blister,
But the certain standard measured and known
By which a man might re-make his soul though all walls were
    down
And all earth's pedestalled gods thrown.

VIII

Sitting on a wooden gate,
Sitting on a wooden gate,
Sitting on a wooden gate
He didnt care a damn.
Said whatever came into his head,
Said whatever came into his head,
Said whatever came into his head
And inconsequently sang.
Inconsequently sang
While his world withered away,
He had a cigarette to smoke and a pound to spend
On drink the next Saturday.
His cattle were fat
And his horses all that
Mid-summer grass could make them.
The young women ran wild
And dreamed of a child
Joy dreams though the fathers might forsake them
But no one would take them,
No one would take them;
No man could ever see
That their skirts had loosed buttons,

12

Deliberately loosed buttons.
O the men were as blind as could be.
And Patrick Maguire
From his purgatory fire
Called the gods of the Christian to prove
That this twisted skein
Was the necessary pain
And not the rope that was strangling true love.

But sitting on a wooden gate
Sometime in July
When he was thirty four or five
He gloried in the lie;
He made it read the way it should,
He made life read the evil good
While he cursed the ascetic brotherhood
Without knowing why.
Sitting on a wooden gate
All, all alone
He sang and laughed
Like a man quite daft,
Or like a man on a channel raft
He fantasied forth his groan.
Sitting on a wooden gate,
Sitting on a wooden gate,
Sitting on a wooden gate
He rode in day-dream cars.
He locked his body with his knees
When the gate swung too much in the breeze.
But while he caught high ecstasies
Life slipped between the bars.

IX

He gave himself another year,
Something was bound to happen before then —
The circle would break down
And he would curve the new one to his own will.
A new rhythm is a new life

And in it marriage is hung and money.
He would be a new man walking through unbroken meadows
Of dawn in the year of One.

The poor peasant talking to himself in a stable door —
An ignorant peasant deep in dung.
What can the passers-by think otherwise?
Where is his silver bowl of knowledge hung?
Why should men be asked to believe in a soul
That is only the mark of a hoof in guttery gaps?
A man is what is written on the label.
And the passing world stares but no one stops
To look closer. So back to the growing crops
And the ridges he never loved.
Nobody will ever know how much tortured poetry the pulled
  weeds on the ridge wrote
Before they withered in the July sun,
Nobody will ever read the wild, sprawling, scrawling mad
  woman's signature,
The hysteria and the boredom of the enclosed nun of his
  thought.
Like the after-birth of a cow stretched on a branch in the wind
Life dried in the veins of these women and men:
The grey and grief and unlove,
The bones in the backs of their hands,
And the chapel pressing its low ceiling over them.

Sometimes they did laugh and see the sunlight,
A narrow slice of divine instruction.
Going along the river at the bend of Sunday
The trout played in the pools encouragement
To jump in love though death bait the hook.
And there would be girls sitting on the grass banks of lanes.
Stretch-legged and lingering staring —
A man might take one of them if he had the courage.
But "No" was in every sentence of their story
Except when the publichouse came in and shouted its piece.

The yellow buttercups and the bluebells among the whinbushes
On rocks in the middle of ploughing

Was a bright spoke in the wheel
Of the peasant's mill.
The goldfinches on the railway paling were worth looking at —
A man might imagine then
Himself in Brazil and these birds the Birds of Paradise
And the Amazon and the romance traced on the school map
    lived again.

Talk in evening corners and under trees
Was like an old book found in a king's tomb.
The children gathered round like students and listened
And some of the saga defied the draught in the open tomb
And was not blown.

X

Their intellectual life consisted in reading
Reynolds' News or the Sunday Dispatch
With sometimes an old almanac brought down from the ceiling
Or a school reader brown with the droppings of thatch.
The sporting results or the headlines or war
Was a humbug profound as the high-brow's Arcana.
Pat tried to be wise to the abstraction of all that
But its secret dribbled down his waistcoat like a drink from a
    strainer.
He wagered a bob each way on the Derby,
He got a straight tip from a man in a shop —
A double from the Guineas it was and thought himself
A master mathematician when one of them came up
And he could explain how much he'd have drawn
On the double if the second leg had followed the first.
He was betting on form and breeding, he claimed,
And the man that did that could never be burst.
After that they went on to the war, and the generals
On both sides were shown to be stupid as hell.
If he's taken *that* road, they remarked of a Marshal,
He'd have . . . O they know their geography well.
This was their university. Maguire was an undergraduate
Who dreamed from his lowly position of rising

To a professorship like Larry McKenna or Duffy
Or the pig-gelder Nallon whose knowledge was amazing.
"A treble, full multiple odds . . . That's flat porter . . .
My turnips are destroyed with the blackguardly crows . . .
Another one . . . No, you're wrong about that thing I was telling
    you . . .
Did you part with your filly , Jack? I heard that you sold her . . .
The students were all savants by the time of pub-close.

XI

A year passed and another hurried after it
And Patrick Maguire was still six months behind life —
His mother six months ahead of it;
His sister straddle-legged across it: —
One leg in hell and the other in heaven
And between the purgatory of middle-aged virginity —
She prayed for release to heaven or hell.
His mother's voice grew thinner like a rust-worn knife
But it cut more venomously as it thinned,
It cut him up the middle till he became more woman than man,
And it cut through to his mind before the end.

Another field whitened in the April air
And the harrows rattled over the seed,
He gathered the loose stones off the ridges carefully
And grumbled to his men to hurry. He looked like a man who
    could give advice
To foolish young fellows. He was forty seven,
And there was depth in his jaw and his voice was the voice of a
    great cattle-dealer,
A man with whom the fair-green gods break even.
"I think I ploughed that lea the proper depth,
She ought to give a crop if any land gives . .
Drive slower with the foal-mare, Joe"
Joe, a young man of imagined wives,
Smiled to himself and answered like a slave:
"You needn't fear or fret.
I'm taking her as easy, as easy as . . .
Easy there Fanny, easy pet."

16

They loaded the day-scoured implements on the cart
As the shadows of poplars crookened the furrows.
It was the evening, evening. Patrick was forgetting to be lonely
As he used to be in Aprils long ago.
It was the menopause, the misery-pause.

The school-girls passed his house laughing every morning
And sometimes they spoke to him familiarly —
He had an idea. School-girls of thirteen
Would see no political intrigue in an old man's friendship.
Love
The heifer waiting to be nosed by the old bull.
That notion passed too — there was the danger of talk
And jails are narrower than the five-sod ridge
And colder than the black hills facing Armagh in February.
He sinned over the warm ashes again and his crime
The law's long arm could not serve with 'time.'

His face set like an old judge's pose:
Respectability and righteousness,
Stand for no nonsense.
The priest from the altar called Patrick Maguire's name
To hold the collecting box in the chapel door
During all the Sundays of May.
His neighbours envied him his holy rise,
But he walked down from the church with affected indifference
And took the measure of heaven angle-wise.

He still could laugh and sing,
But not the wild laugh or the abandoned harmony now
That called the world to new silliness from the top of a wooden
    gate
When thirty five could take the sparrow's bow.
Let us be kind, let us be kind and sympathetic:
Maybe life is not for joking or for finding happiness in —
This tiny light in Oriental Darkness
Looking out chance windows of poetry or prayer.

And the grief and defeat of men like these peasants
Is God's way — maybe — and we must not want too much

To see.
The twisted thread is stronger than the wind-swept fleece.
And in the end who shall rest in truth's high peace?
Or whose is the world now, even now?
O let us kneel where the blind ploughman kneels
And learn to live without despairing
In a mud-walled space —
Illiterate, unknown and unknowing.
Let us kneel where he kneels
And feel what he feels.

One day he saw a daisy and he thought it
Reminded him of his childhood —
He stopped his cart to look at it.
Was there a fairy hiding behind it?

He helped a poor woman whose cow
Had died on her;
He dragged home a drunken man on a winter's night;
And one rare moment he heard the young people playing on the
    railway stile
And he wished them happiness and whatever they most desired
    from life.

He saw the sunlight and begrudged no man
His share of what the miserly soil and soul
Gives in a season to a ploughman.
And he cried for his own loss one late night on the pillow
And yet thanked the God who had arranged these things.

Was he then a saint?
A Mat Talbot of Monaghan?

His sister Mary Anne spat poison at the children
Who sometimes came to the door selling raffle tickets
For holy funds.
"Get out you little tramps" she would scream
As she shook to the hens an apronful of crumbs
But Patrick often put his hand deep down
In his trouser-pocket and fingered out a penny

Or maybe a tobacco-stained caramel.
"You're soft" said the sister "with other people's money
It's not a bit funny."

The cards are shuffled and the deck
Laid flat for cutting — Tom Malone
Cut for trump. I think we'll make
This game, the last, a tanner one.
Hearts. Right. I see you're breaking
Your two year-old. Play quick, Maguire,
The clock there says it half-past ten —
Kate, throw another sod on that fire.
One of the card-players laughs and spits
Into the flame across a shoulder.
Outside, a noise like a rat
Among the hen-roosts. The cock crows over
The frosted townland of the night.
Eleven o'clock and still the game
Goes on and the players seem to be
Drunk in an Orient opium den.
Mid-night, one o'clock, two.
Somebody's leg has fallen asleep.
What about home? Maguire are you
Using your double-tree this week?
Why? do you want it? Play the ace.
There's it, and that's the last card for me.
A wonderful night, we had. Duffy's place
Is very convenient. Is that a ghost or a tree?
And so they go home with dragging feet
And their voices rumble like laden carts.
And they are happy as the dead or sleeping . . .
I should have led that ace of hearts.

XII

The fields were bleached white,
The wooden tubs full of water
Were white in the winds
That blew through Brannagan's Gap on their way from Siberia;

19

The cows on the grassless heights
Followed the hay that had wings —
The February fodder that hung itself on the black branches
Of the hilltop hedge.
A man stood beside a potato-pit
And clapped his arms
And pranced on the crisp roots
And shouted to warm himself.
Then he buck-leaped about the potatoes
And scooped them into a basket.
He looked like a bucking suck-calf
Whose spine was being tickled.
Sometimes he stared across the bogs
And sometimes he straightened his back and vaguely whistled
A tune that weakened his spirit
And saddened his terrier dog's.
A neighbour passed with a spade on his shoulder
And Patrick Maguire bent like a bridge
Whistled — good morning under his oxter,
And the man the other side of the hedge
Champed his spade on the road at his toes
And talked an old sentimentality
While the wind blew under his clothes.

The mother sickened and stayed in bed all day,
Her head hardly dented the pillow, so light and thin it had worn,
But she still enquired after the household affairs.
She held the strings of her children's Punch and Judy and when
   a mouth opened
It was her truth that the dolls would have spoken
If they hadn't been made of wood and tin —
"Did you open the barn door, Pat, to let the young calves in?"
The priest called to see her every Saturday
And she told him her troubles and fears:
"If Mary Anne was settled I'd die in peace —
I'm getting on in years"
"You were a good woman" said the priest
"And your children will miss you when you're gone.
The likes of you this parish never knew,
I'm sure they'll not forget the work you've done."

She reached five bony crooks under the tick —
"Five pounds for Masses — won't you say them quick."
She died one morning in the beginning of May
And a shower of sparrow-notes was the litany for her dying.
The holy water was sprinkled on the bed-clothes
And her children stood around the bed and cried because it was
    too late for crying.
A mother dead! The tired sentiment:
"Mother mother" was a shallow pool
Where sorrow hardly could wash its feet . . .
Mary Anne came away from the deathbed and boiled the calves
    their gruel.
O what was I doing when the procession passed?
Where was I looking?
Young women and men
And I might have joined them.
Who bent the coin of my destiny
That it stuck in the slot?
I remember a night we walked
Through the moon of Donaghmoyne,
Four of us seeking adventure —
It was mid-summer forty years ago.
Now I know
The moment that gave the turn to my life.
O Christ! I am locked in a stable with pigs and cows forever.

XIII

The world looks on
And talks of the peasant:
The peasant has no worries;
In his little lyrical fields
He ploughs and sows;
He eats fresh food,
He loves fresh women,
He is his own master
As it was in the Beginning
The simpleness of peasant life.
The birds that sing for him are eternal choirs,

Everywhere he walks there are flowers.
His heart is pure,
His mind is clear,
He can talk to God as Moses and Isaiah talked —
The peasant who is only one remove from the beasts he drives.
The travellers stop their cars to gape over the green bank into
    his fields: —

There is the source from which all cultures rise,
And all religions,
There is the pool in which the poet dips
And the musician.
Without the peasant base civilisation must die,
Unless the clay is in the mouth the singer's singing is useless.
The travellers touch the roots of the grass and feel renewed
When they grasp the steering wheels again.
The peasant is the unspoiled child of Prophecy,
The peasant is all virtues — let us salute him without irony
The peasant ploughman who is half a vegetable —
Who can re-act to sun and rain and sometimes even
Regret that the Maker of Light had not touched him more
    intensely.
Brought him up from the sub-soil to an existence
Of conscious joy. He was not born blind.
He is not always blind: Sometimes the cataract yields
To sudden stone-falling or the desire to breed.

The girls pass along the roads
And he can remember what man is,
But there is nothing he can do.
Is there nothing he can do?
Is there no ecape?
No escape, no escape.

The cows and horses breed,
And the potato-seed
Gives a bud and a root and rots
In the good mother's way with her sons;
The fledged bird is thrown
From the nest — on its own.

22

But the peasant in his little acres is tied
To a mother's womb by the wind-toughened navel-cord
Like a goat tethered to the stump of a tree —
He circles around and around wondering why it should be.
No crash,
No drama.
That was how his life happened.
No mad hooves galloping in the sky,
But the weak, washy way of true tragedy —
A sick horse nosing around the meadow for a clean place to die.

XIV

We may come out into the October reality, Imagination,
The sleety wind no longer slants to the black hill where Maguire
And his men are now collecting the scattered harness and baskets.
The dog sitting on a wisp of dry stalks
Watches them through the shadows.
"Back in, back in." One talks to the horse as to a brother.
Maguire himself is patting a potato-pit against the weather —
An old man fondling a new-piled grave:
"Joe, I hope you didn't forget to hide the spade
For there's rogues in the townland. Hide it flat in a furrow.
I think we ought to be finished by to-morrow."
Their voices through the darkness sound like voices from a cave,
A dull thudding far away, futile, feeble far away,
First cousins to the ghosts of the townland.

A light stands in a window. Mary Anne
Has the table set and the tea-pot waiting in the ashes.
She goes to the door and listens and then she calls
From the top of the haggard-wall:
"What's keeping you
And the cows to be milked and all the other work there's to do?"
"Alright, alright
We'll not stay here all night."
Applause, applause,
The curtain falls.
Applause, applause

From the homing carts and the trees
And the bawling cows at the gates.
From the screeching water-hens
And the mill-race heavy with the Lammas floods curving over
    the weir.
A train at the station blowing off steam
And the hysterical laughter of the defeated everywhere.
Night, and the futile cards are shuffled again.
Maguire spreads his legs over the impotent cinders that wake no
    manhood now
And he hardly looks to see which card is trump.
His sister tightens her legs and her lips and frizzles up
Like the wick of an oil-less lamp.
The curtain falls
Applause, applause.

Maguire is not afraid of death, the Church will light him a
    candle
To see his way through the vaults and he'll understand the
Quality of the clay that dribbles over his coffin.
He'll know the names of the roots that climb down to tickle his
    feet.
And he will feel no different than when he walked through
    Donaghmoyne.
If he stretches out a hand — a wet clod,
If he opens his nostrils — a dungy smell;
If he opens his eyes once in a million years —
Through a crack in the crust of the earth he may see a face
    nodding in
Or a woman's legs. Shut them again for that sight is sin.

He will hardly remember that life happened to him —
Something was brighter a moment. Somebody sang in the
    distance.
A procession passed down a mesmerised street.
He remembers names like Easter and Christmas
By the colour his fields were.
Maybe he will be born again, a bird of an angel's conceit
To sing the gospel of life
To a music as flightily tangent

As a tune on an oboe.
And the serious look of the fields will have changed to the leer
   of a hobo
Swaggering celestially home to his three wishes granted.
Will that be? will that be?
Or is the earth right that laughs: haw haw
And does not believe
In an unearthly law.
The earth that says:
Patrick Maguire, the old peasant, can neither be damned nor
   glorified:
The graveyard in which he will lie will be just a deep-drilled
   potato-field
Where the seed gets no chance to come through
To the fun of the sun.
The tongue in his mouth is the root of a yew.
Silence, silence. The story is done.

He stands in the doorway of his house
A ragged sculpture of the wind
October creaks the rotted mattress
The bedposts fall. No hope. No. No lust.
The hungry fiend
Screams the apocalypse of clay
In every corner of this land.

TEXTUAL NOTE

Patrick Kavanagh's 'The Great Hunger' first appeared in the English journal, *Horizon*, in January 1942 under the title, 'The Old Peasant'. Only Parts I, II, III and a section of Part IV were printed on this occasion. The entire poem was first published by the Cuala Press in a limited, numbered edition of 250 copies in April 1942. A bowdlerized version, omitting lines 9 to 32 of Part II, was the concluding poem in Kavanagh's second volume of poems, *A Soul For Sale*, published by Macmillans, London, in 1947. The complete poem was not reissued until the publication of Patrick Kavanagh's *Collected Poems* by MacGibbon & Kee, London, in 1964. It has subsequently been included in several poetry anthologies and collected in Patrick Kavanagh, *The Complete Poems*, published by the Peter Kavanagh Hand Press, New York, 1972.

Although 'The Great Hunger' is now widely available, all reprintings since 1964 have been based on the *Collected Poems* version. Yet there are numerous variations, some minor, some significant, between this version and both earlier editions of the poem. Since *Collected Poems* was compiled without Patrick Kavanagh's editorial advice or assistance such variants were introduced without his authorization. This is the first reissue of the original Cuala Press edition of 'The Great Hunger', the only complete version to have been sanctioned by the poet.

Parts I, II and III of 'The Old Peasant' closely resemble the first three parts of the Cuala Press edition of 'The Great Hunger'; Part IV contains only the first three stanzas, the latter two of which were substantially rewritten. Bowdlerization and some changes in spelling and punctuation apart, differences between the Cuala Press and the *A Soul for Sale* texts of the poem are few: two omissions and three verbal substitutions. In *A Soul for Sale* line 6 of Part VI stops after 'complete' and line 23 of Part VIII has been dropped. In Part I 'The horse lifts its head and cranes'; in Part XIV 'The bedposts fall. No hope. No lust.' Occasional eccentricities in punctuation and spelling in the Cuala edition, especially a tendency to excessive hyphenation, are regularized. The *Collected Poems* edition of 'The Great Hunger' is based on the *A Soul for Sale* text but with the bowdlerized passage from Part II restored. However, it also introduces a number of other changes. In addition to an obvious misprint in Part IX, corrected in later reprintings, it drops line 9 from Part VIII; omits a word in five instances and changes a word in four other instances, a significant example being the substitution of 'armful' for 'apronful' in Part XI. Despite these and other unauthorized revisions in punctuation and

27

structural division, the *Collected Poems* version of 'The Great Hunger', because it has been copied in all subsequent publications of the poem, has begun to acquire the status of a definitive text.

If Patrick Kavanagh had his way, of course, 'The Great Hunger' would not have been reissued. He repudiated it on several occasions, most notoriously in his 'Author's Note' to *Collected Poems*. Disparaging its 'kinetic vulgarity' and its social concern, he dismissed the poem as 'tragedy' and defined tragedy as 'underdeveloped Comedy, not fully born'. Whatever the author's opinion of its demerits, however, 'The Great Hunger' is generally acclaimed as one of his finest poetic achievements and a masterpiece of modern Irish literature. Now, almost half a century after its first publication, the original version of the poem is at long last available to Kavanagh's many readers.

Dr Antoinette Quinn
Trinity College, Dublin

Tom Mac Intyre
THE GREAT HUNGER

from the poem
by Patrick Kavanagh

The Great Hunger was first performed by the Abbey Theatre Company at the Peacock Theatre, Dublin, on Monday, 9 May 1983, when the cast was as follows:

MAGUIRE	Tom Hickey
PRIEST	Vincent O'Neill
TOM MALONE	Conal Kearney
MARY ANNE	Bríd ní Neachtain
AGNES	Fiona MacAnna
SCHOOL GIRL	Martina Stanley

The play was directed by Patrick Mason and designed by Bronwen Casson.

Some reviews of the 1986 Abbey Theatre Production:

'This is one of the greatest things that the Edinburgh Festival and fringe have ever seen . . . a realization on stage of Patrick Kavanagh's poem of 1942 . . . a masterpiece of script, direction, design and performance.'

Owen Dudley Edwards in *The Scotsman.*

'A towering example of how drama can work through image and gesture as well as speech.'

Michael Billington in *The Guardian.*

'As experimental and original as anything by Samuel Beckett . . . I realized I was in the presence of a modern masterpiece of compassion about the deprived and pathetically faint of heart.'

John Barber in *The Daily Telegraph.*

NOTE

For Tom Hickey

Setting
Loosely defined, fluid as possible. Three main areas. Outdoors is placed centrally – it is marked only by a wooden gate, far upstage. The kitchen and chapel areas: place downstage left and right, respectively. THE MOTHER will usually be found in the kitchen area; place there, also, a large black kettle and a bucket. The chapel is distinguished by a tabernacle resting on its pedestal.

Duration
A little over one hundred minutes; the piece is played, ideally, without an interval.

Participants
MAGUIRE
THE MOTHER (a wooden effigy)
THE SISTER, MARY ANNE
THE PRIEST
AGNES
THE SCHOOL-GIRL
TOM MALONE
PACKY
JOE

EXTRA MALE
YOUNG WOMEN

The piece may be played by six players,
three female and three male.

Scene One

Wind sounds, harsh. Fading as MAGUIRE *appears.* MAGUIRE *wandering the space, bent forward slightly, arms folded across his chest, hands beating shoulders.*

MAGUIRE   The bridge is too narrow . . . . The bridge is too narrow and the hay has wings.

PACKY   (*off*) Maguire . . . Maguire . . .

MAGUIRE   And thirty-five could take the sparrow's bow . . .

PACKY   Maguire . . . Maguire . . .

MAGUIRE   You're wrong . . . . You're wrong about that thing I was tellin' you, you're wrong, you're wrong . . .

PACKY   Maguire . . . Maguire . . .

MAGUIRE   The tubs is white . . . . The tubs is white . . . . The tubs is white . . .

PACKY *enters upstage right with lantern, lit. Crosses upstage of the gate to exit upstage left.*

PACKY   Maguire, you're wrong about that thing I was tellin' you, Maguire, you're wrong, you're wrong . . .

MAGUIRE   We ought to be finished by the morrow . . .

MAGUIRE *looks about him as if coming out of sleep, removes glasses, wipes eyes with closed fists, enters the daylight world.*

Scene Two

Two of MAGUIRE's *men,* MALONE *and* JOE, *enter upstage left. They carry spades, and, between them, a metal bath. It contains three metal buckets and a bag-apron. The bath is set downstage left, as is the bag-apron.* MALONE *and* JOE *go to the head of the potato drills where* MAGUIRE *joins them. The buckets have been distributed. The potato-picking commences.*

PACKY *has also entered upstage left, and settled on the gate. From there he watches the action.*

Girlish laughter off. The men give no heed.

MAGUIRE *erupts. Something spotted in the next field. He whistles for the dog. No dog to be had.*

MAGUIRE   Curse o' God, where's that dog? Never where he's wanted.

A burst of shouting from MAGUIRE, *and wild mime of pegging stones. As they work, the three converse.*

MAGUIRE   Move forward the basket —
JOE   The wind's over Brannigan's —
MAGUIRE   Balance it steady —
JOE   That means rain —
MALONE   Down the ruckety pass —
MAGUIRE   The wind's over Brannigan's —
JOE   That means rain —
MALONE   Down the ruckety pass —
MAGUIRE   Pull down the shafts of that cart, Joe —
JOE   And straddle the horse —
MAGUIRE   And straddle the horse —
MALONE   Down the ruckety pass —
MAGUIRE   Graip up some withered stalks, graip up some withered stalks and see that no potato falls —
JOE   Over the tailboard —
MAGUIRE   Over the tailboard —
MALONE   Down the ruckety pass —
MAGUIRE   Going down the ruckety pass. And that's a job, that's a job we'll have to do in December —
JOE   Gravel it —
MAGUIRE   Gravel it and build a kerb —
MALONE   Down the ruckety pass —
JOE   And build a kerb —
MAGUIRE   Gravel it and build a kerb on the bog side —

36

MALONE   On the bog side —

Burst of girlish laughter off, and one runs on, downstage right, 'Will-I-won't-I' demeanour. Runs downstage of the men to leapfrog over JOE, *and – full tilt – exit upstage left.*

The heads of the men dive – Three heads hanging between wide-apart legs – to see. Too late. Slowly they rise from that position and become scarecrows stirring lightly in the wind, scarecrows that swivel and stare vacantly into the audience.

PACKY, *watcher on the gate, chants.*

PACKY   Ploughs and sows .... Eats fresh food .... Loves fresh women .... His own master – can talk to God.

The men at work again, bringing the full buckets to empty the potatoes into the bath.

MAGUIRE   Never where he's wanted —

MALONE *and* JOE *exit upstage right with bath, buckets, spades.* PACKY *is exiting upstage left as* MAGUIRE *playfully skelps a couple of potatoes off the back wall.* MAGUIRE *dons his bag-apron and moves downstage right as* MARY ANNE *enters stage right.*

Scene Three

MAGUIRE   Patrick Maguire went home and made cocoa .... The sister, the sister – hens and calves, calves and hens ...

MARY ANNE *arrives downstage left carrying a large black kettle and an enamel bucket containing water. She leaves down kettle and bucket and moves to a position upstage and stage right of* THE MOTHER. *She stares* MAGUIRE *who's still downstage right.* MAGUIRE *responds by crossing to* THE MOTHER *and making an irritated attempt to loosen the cord which binds the cover about her.* MARY ANNE *turns her back on him, faces upstage.* MAGUIRE *moves downstage to occupy himself pouring water from bucket to kettle. The two share another look.* MAGUIRE *approaches* THE MOTHER. *A second time, claws at the cord. Fails to loosen it.* MARY ANNE *intervenes, sweeps towards him with scissors aloft, snips. Returns to her position, again gives her back to the proceedings.*

The cord is now in MAGUIRE's *control. He loosens it all the way by running circles about* THE MOTHER. *Cord free, and dumped on the ground.* MAGUIRE *gives his attention to the cover, frees it – but not without making work for himself. Flings sheet on the ground in turn.*

MARY ANNE *spins to face him. Goes forward to gather cord and cover – briskly, neatly, and places both downstage in line with bucket and kettle. That done, she returns to her position upstage of* THE MOTHER. *She again faces upstage but her stance is mitigated. A hint of the diagonal gives her a sightline to the downstage left area.*

MAGUIRE *goes to the* (MOTHER-) *drawer, opens it, takes out a wire brush and a duster. He throws the brush to* MARY ANNE. *She catches it, moves downstage left and starts cleaning the kettle, first removing the lid.*

MAGUIRE *busies himself cleaning* THE MOTHER's *face, talking to her at the start, shouting before long.*

MAGUIRE	No, no, the pig-gelder Nallon —
MARY ANNE	What's keeping you? Did you let the hens out you?
MAGUIRE	No —
MARY ANNE	Did you open the barn door? Let the young calves in?
MAGUIRE	The pig-gelder, the pig-gelder?
MARY ANNE	What's *he* looking for there?
MAGUIRE	*Nallon —*
MARY ANNE	Brazil and The Amazon —
MAGUIRE	The pig-gelder Nallon —
MARY ANNE	Brazil and The Amazon —
MAGUIRE	The pig-gelder Nallon —
MARY ANNE	Poor Paddy Maguire —
MAGUIRE	*Nallon —*

MARY ANNE	The great cattle-dealer hobo —
MAGUIRE	Nallon, *Nallon, Nallon* —

MAGUIRE *pitches the duster into the drawer, kicks the drawer shut.*
MARY ANNE *slams the lid on the kettle and throws the wire brush to*
MAGUIRE. *He catches it. Extended pause as they stare each other.*
MAGUIRE *then to the drawer. Opens it, tosses the wire brush into it,*
closes the drawer. Looks again at MARY ANNE.

MARY ANNE *will not be rushed. She stoops, rests her hands on the*
kettle, releases a sigh.

MAGUIRE, *downstage right of* THE MOTHER, *flops to the floor, sits*
with his back to THE MOTHER, *legs extended, repetitively banging his*
feet together. He converses with MARY ANNE *by that mode.*

She converses with him by her mode of pouring water very slowly
from bucket to kettle. Squeaks from the bucket handle are an aid to
articulation. She takes forever at pouring the water.

Bucket empty, MARY ANNE *replaces lid on kettle, settles kettle and*
bucket — and cord and cover, moves upstage to THE MOTHER, *checks*
THE MOTHER's *face, and exits downstage left. During that series of*
movements, she communes with herself.

MARY ANNE	Pigs and cows, Punch and Judy . . . Punch and
	Judy, pigs and cows . . . Nallon . . . . The pig-
	gelder Nallon . . .

MAGUIRE *senses her exit, stops his feet-banging. Listens. Rises and*
goes to the drawer. Opens it. Interrupts himself to remove the bag-
apron and place it downstage, a prayer-mat of sorts. Returns to the
drawer, takes from it a bellows. With the bellows, goes to the bag-
apron. Kneels. Tentatively works the bellows, then works it to climax
in an image of masturbation.

He returns the bellows to the drawer, shuts the drawer. Goes to the
kettle and pours from the kettle back into the bucket, pouring that
releases The Isle of Capri *on the sound track. Quality of the recording*
to suggest the uncertain radio in the farmhouse back of the hills.

39

Scene Four

Enter MALONE *upstage right, waltzing to the music. He settles upstage of the gate, leaning across it.* MAGUIRE *joins him there.* MAGUIRE *playfully belts* MALONE *with his cap, and there's a dance between them which develops that greeting. Finally, the two yield to the enjoyment of staring into emptiness.*

THREE YOUNG WOMEN *enter, variously, settle downstage right. Vivaciously, they daub their mouths with lipstick, perfume themselves. The three play with these phrases . . . If he opens his eyes . . . if he opens, opens, opens . . . sight is sin . . . if he opens legs . . . a face in the crust . . . legs, legs, legs . . .*

MAGUIRE *and* MALONE, *swiping at midges, have turned their backs to the action.*
 As THE YOUNG WOMEN *get into their stride,* AGNES *declaims —*

> AGNES Sittin' on a wooden gate, sittin' on a wooden gate, sittin' on a wooden gate, he didn't give a damn . . . . Said whatever came into his head, said whatever came into his head, said whatever came into his head, he didn't give a damn.

THE PRIEST *enters, upstage right, a fraction after* THE YOUNG WOMEN, *and makes for the downstage left area. First he goes to the kettle, taps it several times with polished toe. Next the bucket. He stoops, taken by his reflection in the water, adjusts his collar.*

Now he approaches THE MOTHER. *He studies her. Takes out a small mirror and holds it to her mouth. The breath-stain is faint, it seems . . . . He moves his index finger across her line of vision. Yes, she's alive. He takes off his hat and rests it on her lap. He goes to her right ear and bawls into it. We hear nothing. Repeat. This time we hear.*

> THE PRIEST Your children will miss you when you're gone.

At intervals, MAGUIRE *and* MALONE *flail at the midges, fall into their torpor again.*

THE PRIEST *now turns entertainer, does a card-trick for* THE MOTHER. *He offers a running commentary of sounds rather than words. Card-trick over,* THE PRIEST *gives himself to listening, head bowed, to* THE MOTHER. *A confession moment, could be. Thus positioned,* THE PRIEST *falls asleep.*

The moment of THE PRIEST'S *dropping off brings* PACKY *racing on, blades of grass held to his lips to form a makeshift whistle— which he works to resonant effect. He delivers a blast to the tabernacle, a blast to* THE MOTHER, *then races off.*

THE YOUNG WOMEN *respond to his incursion by placing their palms, crossed, in front of their faces. His exit releases them. They jump to their feet and flash lights over the audience from hand-mirrors they manoeuvre. Next they flash the mirrors at* MAGUIRE *and* MALONE *upstage of the gate. And they shout at the men.*

YOUNG WOMEN   What's keeping you? And the cows to be milked
                and all the other work there's to do. We'll not
                stay here all night.

They exit, variously. One of them, noticing THE PRIEST'S *hat on the lap of* THE MOTHER, *grabs it and slaps it on* THE MOTHER'S *head.*

The teasing of THE YOUNG WOMEN *stirs* MAGUIRE *and* MALONE *to further flailing at the midges, no more than that.*

THE PRIEST *rouses from his sleep. Looks about him. Spots his hat on the head of* THE MOTHER. *Smiles for her. Takes his hat and dons it. Speaks to* THE MOTHER.

    THE PRIEST   The likes of you this parish never knew.

He exits upstage right.

MAGUIRE *and* MALONE *stir themselves.* MAGUIRE *takes out a cigarette and lights up.* MALONE *– gasping for a drag – cadges the cigarette. The pair puff contentedly.*

The summer evening light yields to night. Glow of the cigarettes by the gate, glow of one cigarette answering the other, that conversation.

The two make for home.

> MAGUIRE Is that a ghost or a tree?
> MALONE Down the ruckety pass —
> MAGUIRE Duffy's place is very convenient.
> MALONE A wonderful night we had.

MAGUIRE *and* MALONE *exit downstage right.*

Scene Five

A spring moment of release. Brilliant lighting, triumphant music – but finding its way, prelude as yet. MALONE *enters downstage right,* PACKY *upstage left. They each carry piles of green-leaved branches which they dump centre-stage. And off.*

Now all the players – bar THE PRIEST *– enter and take possession of the branches. The green branch is magic. For each an individual way of dealing with it.* MAGUIRE *is ecstatic,* MARY ANNE *severe.* THE SCHOOL-GIRL *is rapt, squeezing the leaves, raising her hand to drink the odours;* AGNES *lies down and, laughing, strokes the branches against thighs, breasts, face;* MALONE *is tearing off leaves, pocketing them happily;* PACKY *finds gestures at once grotesque and fragile to convey his delight.*

A tremendous stir and the music rising in intensity. MAGUIRE, MARY ANNE, *and* MALONE *fuss about* THE MOTHER. *A branch for her also. The cover – as rug – about her shoulders. Procession imminent. The music peaks, and they process about the space.* THE SCHOOL-GIRL *dips her branch in the bucket, blesses each player in turn, blesses the audience.*

> SCHOOL-GIRL Holy Spirit is the rising sap . . . Holy Spirit is the
> rising sap . . .

The space is drumming exuberance.

THE PRIEST *enters downstage right. Everything stops.* THE PRIEST *removes the cover from the tabernacle. The players discard the branches and assemble (*THE MOTHER *is brought alone) in the 'chapel' area, kneeling positions.*

PACKY, *as altar-boy, is downstage right, close to* THE PRIEST. AGNES *is in the 'front row', flirtatious in her concentration on* THE PRIEST. *Next comes* MARY ANNE *and* THE MOTHER. *Thereafter,* THE SCHOOL-GIRL, MALONE, *and, downstage left,* MAGUIRE.

To start, there's an orchestrated din of coughing which turns to a chorale of farmyard noises, animal and fowl. This rises wildly so that THE PRIEST *is forced to exercise control. A signal to* PACKY, *and* PACKY *jingles a minatory bell. The din subsides.*

Prayers: From the dialogue snippets below, surreal antiphonal exchanges are developed between THE PRIEST *and the congregation, and between members of the congregation.*

Remember Eileen Farrelly? I was thinking a man might do a damn sight worse.

She ought to give a crop if any land gives.

Wonder should I cross-plough that turnip ground?

Is that Cassidy's ass out in my clover?

The wind's over Brannigan's, that means rain.

Did you part with your filly, Jack?

Kate, throw another sod on that fire.

Get out, you little tramps.

Easy there, Fanny, easy pet.

43

Back in, back in, and you'll have all the luck.

Curse o' God, where's that dog?

Drive slower with the foal mare, Joe.

My turnips are destroyed with the blackguardly crows.

Hop back there, Polly, hoy back, woa, wae, *is used as reiterated* Amen.

A precise signal from THE PRIEST *concludes prayers. He allows a silence to shape. Searches in the folds of his vestments for the tabernacle key. Roots in his pockets. Key not to be found – until an embarrassed* PACKY *produces it from his pocket.* THE PRIEST (*with a look of chastisement for* PACKY) *takes the key, kisses it. Addresses himself to the tabernacle door. Insertion of the key in the lock. Turning of the key. Opening of the door. Curtains of red silk visible. Delicately,* THE PRIEST *parts these. He takes out a small dingy chalice, tarnished, but it contains the mystery. He extends it to the congregation. Worshipful, they yield.*

Break, on the tinkle of a bell from PACKY.

A nod from THE PRIEST *sends* MAGUIRE *into action with the long-handled collection-box. Each contribution is individualized.* AGNES *releases her coins like delectable confections for the priest.* MARY ANNE *defines constriction: tight-lipped. A single coin.* THE SCHOOL-GIRL *becomes a Jack-in-the-Box to* MAGUIRE'S *conducting.* MALONE *contents himself with simply rattling the box.*

Collection completed, MAGUIRE, *passing the bucket, dreamily spills all the coins into the water – as if the most natural thing in the world.*

All stare. MAGUIRE *comes to, stands there.* THE PRIEST *starts laughing – exoneration (maybe). Laughing spreads, threatens to become tumult.* THE PRIEST *cools it with a look.*

PACKY *rings the bell and the mass is over. The congregation scatter.*

THE MOTHER *is taken home,* MARY ANNE, AGNES, THE SCHOOL-GIRL *and* MALONE, *the bearers.*

PACKY *hovers to assist* THE PRIEST's *disrobing.*

MAGUIRE, *rattling a coin in the collection-box, ambiguously his own man, goes up to* THE PRIEST, *gives an absent-minded genuflection, and is moving upstage left to exit when his attention is caught by* AGNES *upstage right.*

THE PRIEST *and* PACKY *are downstage right. Poised.*

AGNES *stares* MAGUIRE, *stare close to the accusatory.* MAGUIRE *is held.* AGNES – *a broad powerful gesture for* MAGUIRE's *assimilation – bangs her fist silently against the back wall. Exits upstage right.* MAGUIRE *exits upstage left.*

And THE PRIEST, PACKY *in attendance, commences disrobing. He hands* PACKY *the biretta, places the maniple on* PACKY's *left arm, robes* PACKY *in the chasuble, quizzing* PACKY *as he does.*

> THE PRIEST Who bent the coin that it stuck in the slot? The brown breeze through the thistles . . . . Through the thistles the brown breeze . . .

THE PRIEST – *elaborately – removes the cincture, which he then spirals into the biretta –* PACKY *observing in fascination.*

> THE PRIEST We must not want too much to know.

On that line, THE PRIEST *pulls a card from the biretta – for* PACKY's *edification and astonishment.*

Exit PACKY *downstage right.*

THE PRIEST *faces the audience, rubs his palms, magics the card out of existence.*

Exit THE PRIEST *upstage right.*

Scene Six

THE SCHOOL-GIRL *on. She flourishes a book of raffle tickets, comes downstage shaking it like a tambourine. She writes, tears off a counterfoil, throws it to the house.*

    SCHOOL-GIRL   For holy funds —

Now she does a figure of eight around THE MOTHER *and tabernacle, writes again, repeats the routine and the line.*
   This brings MAGUIRE *on, jingling coins. She notices. She gestures —* Will you buy? *He will. He comes downstage to her, stands over her, as, resting on one knee, she writes, gives him the counterfoil. He takes it, and — jokey — withholds the money. He jigs about the space, teasing her and generally clowning: animal imitations, fowl imitations. Frustrated, she pitches the book of tickets at him and stalks off.*
   MAGUIRE *changes tack. Shouts after her, halts her. Goes towards her and places the money on the ground and retreats — as she advances — with the book of tickets now in his possession. She collects the money. And he's off into a second round of teasing, flourishing the tickets à la* THE SCHOOL-GIRL *at the start of the scene.*
   MAGUIRE's *teasing romp takes him out of the space — but the noise of the tickets being 'rattled' suggests where he is: downstage right and off. She advances in that direction. The noise leads her on.*
   She peers irritably, hesitates. And MAGUIRE — *squawking — gallops on upstage left. She screeches.* MAGUIRE *again into his fowl imitations — turkey sounds and strutting, goose-hissing and waddling, that idiom.*
   THE SCHOOL-GIRL *in difficulties. She backs off, for a moment. Retaliates by taking up his idiom and challenging him with verve. So: that dance (mirror-game) with a sudden access of mutual enjoyment. The natural climax is that she leaps boldly into his embrace: her arms about his neck, her legs about his waist. The two whirl, brief release, then a jolt. There's a mutual realization of the sexual voltage. The pulse of this commands the space.*
   Slowly, dangerously, THE SCHOOL-GIRL *slides from* MAGUIRE's *embrace, grabs the tickets from him and exits at speed.*
   MAGUIRE *alone, adrift, recovering, not recovering.*

Scene Seven

Evening at the crossroads . . . MAGUIRE *joined by* MALONE, JOE *and* PACKY. *The four commence a desultory game of pitch-and-toss – horse-play an element – which yields quickly to the following sequence: the players' recollections of* The Mucker Dramatic Society's *last presentation, the recollections taking the shape of line-swopping with a competitive tilt.*

As the game of pitch-and-toss disintegrates, MARY ANNE *enters downstage left and hunkers by* THE MOTHER. *She has a jar of Pond's Cold Cream. Patiently, dreamily, she rubs cream on her hands and neck.*

MAGUIRE *sets the line-swopping in motion –*

> MAGUIRE God the Father . . . God the Father . . . God the Father in a tree . . . ?

MALONE *takes up the challenge –*

> MALONE God is in the bits . . . God is in the bits . . . God is in the bits and pieces of . . . ?

PACKY *is suddenly a target. The others advance demandingly on him:* PACKY, *gawky/girlish, is there to be teased, to be murkily desired.*

> MAG/MAL/JOE Of? Of? Of? Of?
> PACKY Of every day –

Mockingly, the three interrogators echo PACKY's Of every day. PACKY *retaliates, hesitantly shows his paces, mimes the act of breaking bread as he challenges them to respond.*

> PACKY In a crumb of bread? In a crumb of bread? In a crumb of bread?

The others turn the question back on PACKY, *surrounding him, jostling him.*

> MAG/MAL/JOE Crumb of bread? Crumb of bread? Crumb of bread?

PACKY   The whole mystery is . . .

Again the others echo his answer mockingly.

MAG/MAL/JOE   The *whole* mystery is . . . The *whole* mystery is
. . . The *whole* mystery is . . .

The diversion is taking on intensity, they're all more and more caught in the rhythms of it. MAGUIRE *keeps it moving.*

MAGUIRE   The green leaves? The green leaves? The green
leaves?

He's waving a small branch as he puts the question, jigging about, inviting the others to rush him, tumble him.

MAGUIRE   The green leaves? The green leaves?

The others rush him.

MAG/MAL/JOE   The green leaves? The green leaves? The green
leaves?

They tumble MAGUIRE. *He shouts the answering line as he goes down.*

MAGUIRE   Christ will be the green leaves that will come —
OMNES   Christ will be the green leaves that will come —

That's a signal. They all know the next move. MAGUIRE — *content to wait — drifts downstage, gives himself to a gestural cameo which posits the branch in his possession as the starting-handle of a car.* MALONE *and* JOE, *meanwhile, have been active by the gate. They plank* PACKY *upstage of the gate and move to re-stage the resurrection hour.* MALONE *and* JOE, *downstage right and left of the gate, produce dawn/wind sounds by whirling lengths of wire above their heads.* PACKY *has been climbing the gate. He now stands on it as the risen Christ, arms outstretched, palms spread wide — and focussing on* MAGUIRE, *even as* MAGUIRE *is turning to meet the upstage event.* MAGUIRE, *shaken, takes off his cap. All goes eerily quiet.* MALONE *and* JOE *drop the lengths of wire.* MARY ANNE *speaks into the silence.*

MARY ANNE   Your children'll miss you when you're gone.

MAGUIRE, MALONE, *and* JOE *resume the pitch-and-toss – but the air is changed.* PACKY *remains on the gate, seated.* MARY ANNE *lids the jar of Pond's cream, rises, and – diagonal line through the heedless males – makes her slow exit upstage right.*
Frail echoes of the line-swopping dialogue accompany the resumed pitch-and-toss.

MAGUIRE   God the Father in a tree —
MALONE   God is in the bits —
JOE   In a crumb of bread —
MAGUIRE   God the Father —
MALONE   In the bits —
JOE   Crumb of bread —
MAGUIRE   God —
MALONE   Bits —
JOE   Crumb —

That final 'crumb' cues the sound of a passing train. All listen, immobilized. . . . The sound fades. The pitch-and-toss is beyond recovery – for now. MAGUIRE *– in an evident fever – breaks from the group and exits downstage right. The other three hold separate positions, idly brooding:* PACKY *on the gate,* MALONE *hunkered downstage right,* JOE *standing midstage left between the gate and* THE MOTHER.
MAGUIRE'S *hysterical laughter can be heard off. He spins back on, very near the edge, and careers about the space, repeating —*

MAGUIRE   Patrick Maguire went home and made cocoa . . .

His whirl now finds blurred focus. He approaches PACKY *on the gate, declaring urgently —*

MAGUIRE   Patrick Maguire went home and made cocoa and
broke a chunk off the loaf of wheaten bread . . .

PACKY *makes no response.* MAGUIRE *descends on* JOE—

MAGUIRE   His mother called down to him to look again
and make sure the hen-house was locked . . .

JOE *makes no response.* MAGUIRE *descends on* MALONE —

> MAGUIRE His sister grunted in bed, the sound of a sow
> taking up a new position . . .

MALONE *makes no response.* MAGUIRE — *more and more into vertigo
— is swept wildly about the space, gabbling fragments from the
speeches he has just uttered. He halts, downstage right: tongue
bobbing in and out, hands fluttering in the crotch area, he looses an
image of masturbation. Takes off again,* distrait —

> MAGUIRE Patrick Maguire went home and made cocoa
> and broke a chunk off the loaf of wheaten bread.
> His mother called down to him to look again
> and make sure the hen-house was locked. His
> sister grunted in bed, the sound of a sow taking
> up a new position . . .

*He comes to rest downstage left as we hear the voices of young
women, gabbling easily, passing by . . .*

*All the males listen, cling to the fading sounds. In the silence that
follows, the four stare emptily across the audience and into the
beyond.*

They lurch free of that fog. MALONE *tosses a coin,* JOE *shoulders
him playfully to the ground,* PACKY *pushes* MAGUIRE *on to* MALONE,
MAGUIRE *straddles* MALONE, *and* The Heifer Romp *is away.*

MALONE *as the heifer. Commence with a general inspection, to a
cacophony of groans from the animal. The teeth are checked, the
flanks, the backbone is tickled — the heifer bucks madly — and, for
climax, the hindquarters are feelingly caressed.*

MAGUIRE *fetches a bucket, and —* PACKY *in charge — the heifer is
given a 'drink' from the bucket. More pushing and mauling and
medley of sounds.*

The mounting of the heifer. As PACKY *and the heifer perform their
bucket-dance,* JOE, MAGUIRE *leading him, canters the perimeter,
steadies, and — the hullabaloo reaching peak — moves in and mounts
the waiting heifer. This action develops into a scrum. There's a
writhing of bodies and a sudden lunge for* PACKY — *who exits at speed.*

MAGUIRE   Packy ... Packy ... Packy ...

MAGUIRE, MALONE, *and* JOE, *rise one by one and silently. An exhausted quiet rules.* JOE *exits.* MAGUIRE *and* MALONE *adrift in the aftermath.*

MALONE   What about home?
MAGUIRE   We're too tired to go home yet.
MALONE   Are you using your double-tree this week?
MAGUIRE   Why? D'ye want it?
MALONE   *(exiting)* Why: D'ye want it? Why? D'ye want it? Why? D'ye want it?

MAGUIRE *alone in the space, downstage right. Kneading crumbs of clay. His hands fall idle. He studies his hands ... lifts them fractionally for a better view ... studies his hands ....*

Scene Eight

MAGUIRE *to the gate. He whistles for the dog. No sign of the dog.* MAGUIRE *to the kitchen area. He stands by* THE MOTHER. *Tries to articulate something. Gives up. Opens the (* MOTHER-*) drawer, takes out a duster, wipes* THE MOTHER's *eyes and nose. Tries again to articulate something.*

MAGUIRE   Mother ... Mother ...

He puts the duster away, and, kneeling position, slowly closes the drawer.

THE SCHOOL-GIRL *enters upstage left, picks up a branch as she arrives, and crosses upstage of the gate to exit downstage right. She pulls leaves off the branch as she delivers the lines.*

SCHOOL-GIRL   The poor peasant talking to himself in a stable door, an ignorant peasant deep in dung .... Where is his silver bowl of knowledge hung?

Why should men be asked to believe in a soul
that is only the mark of a hoof in guttery gaps?
A man is what is written . . . . A man is what is
written . . .

As she exits, MAGUIRE *rouses himself. He clutches* THE MOTHER, *leans
his head on her shoulder. With his fist he beats her breast, slowly,
mechanically, the fist beats on the breast of* THE MOTHER.

Scene Nine

*Ploughing. Abrupt switch to an atmosphere of wild release. To
commence: sea-gulls noisily active about the upturned sod. Two of*
THE YOUNG WOMEN, *plus* PACKY, *each with a white table-cloth,
frenetic through the space. And screeching. The third young woman
involved at the same tempo – but as terrier dog, fighting with the
birds, with anything that moves, helplessly taken by the excitement.*

Enter MAGUIRE, *guiding the imaginary plough,* MALONE *and* JOE *as
the horses. Movement – tempestous – back-and-forth in the space.
Intricate gymnastics negotiating the turns at each end – swerve and
sway, sock free, sock plunged again, at intervals impeded by a rock or
whatever . . .*

*The wheeling birds and uncontrollable dog – and the giddy horses –
intensify a persistent sense of the operation threatening to run amok.*
MAGUIRE *has shouts for the horses –*

> MAGUIRE Hop back there, Polly h· ·· ·back, woa, wae. . . .
> Easy there, Fanny, easy pet . . .

*The scene is brief and moves rapidly towards climax – the horses out
of control, and, on the heels of that,* MAGUIRE *and the horses, tangled
on the ground, 'harness' flying in all directions.*

*The sea-gulls vanish, their work done. The terrier – prime
miscreant – delays to piss on the prostrate* MAGUIRE, *vanishes in turn,
yelping delirium.*

The horses – becoming men – laugh as they right themselves.
MAGUIRE, *getting to his feet, is not amused.*

52

MAGUIRE It's not a bit funny . . .

MAGUIRE *kicks the gate several times –*

MAGUIRE Not a bit funny . . . . Not a bit funny . . .

MAGUIRE *collects the 'plough' (a length of wood* suffices) *and the 'harness' (ropes), and places them downstage centre, catching breath, poised for the reward/relaxation of the pub.*

Scene Ten

Three pints of Guinness are waiting on a covered tray downstage right. MALONE *lifts the tray.* JOE *triumphantly removes the cover, and casually places it on* MALONE's *head – a quasi-helmet. Taken by the picture,* JOE *remarks to* MAGUIRE –

JOE Rommel –

MAGUIRE *agrees: there is a likeness. The three – all in possession of their pints by now – play with the word 'Rommel', testing the curiosity – and familiarity – of it. This cadence finds peak in the three raising their pints in a toast –*

OMNES *Rommel –*

The three next move about in close formation, leaning against each other, manoeuvring for positions of maximum comfort before settling into a position where they are adroitly/comfortably propping each other up.

Finding the position of maximum comfort involves a deal of grunt and groan and orchestrated sigh. Finally, contentment. They savour the pints. And they converse: insider talk, seasoned with the inconsequential. MAGUIRE *leads off –*

MAGUIRE She ought to give a crop if any land gives.
JOE They know their geography.

53

MAGUIRE	No one'd take her.
MALONE	That's flat porter.

They drink.

JOE	Me turnips –
MALONE	'Turnips!'
JOE	Me turnips is destroyed with the blackguardly crows.
MAGUIRE	Another one.
MALONE	That's flat porter.

They jostle for more comfort, settle again.

MAGUIRE	Stand for no nonsense –
JOE	There's rogues –
MAGUIRE	Your filly, Jack –
JOE	There's *rogues* –
OMNES	R-o-g-u-e-s . . .
JOE	There's rogues in the townland –
MAGUIRE	Nothin' he could do.
MALONE	That's flat porter.

MAGUIRE *and* JOE *break from the propping-each-up position.* MALONE *lands on the floor.*

MALONE	If the second leg had followed the first –
MAGUIRE	The man could do that'd never be bust.

JOE *and* MALONE *now exiting, upstage right and left, respectively.*

JOE	Like a buckin' suck calf and the winds from Siberia . . .
MAGUIRE	He'd never be bust –
JOE	And the winds from Siberia . . .
MALONE	A treble full multiple odds . . . . Bettin' on form and breedin' . . .

MAGUIRE *alone upstage right – and turning sombre.*

MAGUIRE	The man could do that'd never be bust . . .

Scene Eleven

As MARY ANNE *enters upstage left* MAGUIRE *– facing upstage – is shuffling hesitantly, being sucked towards, the kitchen area.*

MARY ANNE Pigs and cows, Punch and Judy, Punch and Judy, pigs and cows . . .

MARY ANNE *advances on* THE MOTHER *–*

MARY ANNE I'm getting on in years . . . . If Mary Anne was settled I'd die in peace . . . *Amen* . . . . The likes of you . . . . The likes of you . . . .

MAGUIRE *has arrived.* MARY ANNE *turns her wrath on him –*

MARY ANNE *The likes of you –*

MAGUIRE'S *response is immediate. He lies down, angle of 45° to the front-stage line, slaps his cap on his face, and – shamelessly infantile – lifts and lets fall his legs, again and again banging the floor: until* MARY ANNE *intervenes, grabs his upraised feet, swivels him towards* THE MOTHER, *lets his feet fall, gets the bag-apron, and pitches it on him, as who should say –* Now to work, if you're up to it. *That done, she sits down herself, stage left of* THE MOTHER, *removes a shoe, and massages her toes in quiet frenzy.*

MAGUIRE *slides the cap off his face, lifts his head a little, looks at her, muttering and not daring to mutter, garbling the syllables of the word 'mother'.*
MARY ANNE *listens.*
She helps him, as a teacher might, repeating closely, over and over 'mother' . . . 'mother' . . . 'mother' . . . leading him to clearer articulation, steering him until he gets it right. Finally, the word is spewing from him – and from her. He rises, frothing revolt. MARY ANNE *dons her shoe and joins him, companion-rebel, they've played this out before. She pulls out the drawer, spills everything, tosses the drawer one side. He spreads the bag-apron as table-cloth. And they go to it, taking the objects, rags, dusters, the wire-brush, the bellows, and slamming them on to the bag-apron in rising fury. Next: everything*

into the maw of the bag. MARY ANNE *rolls up the bag and slings it to* MAGUIRE — *will he bell the cat?* MAGUIRE *shapes to act, stutters hesitation, crumples, lets the bag fall.*

MARY ANNE, *oozing contempt, gathers it, advances murderously on* THE MOTHER, *raises the loaded bag on high and slams it to the ground directly before* THE MOTHER.

And she exits upstage left.

Scene Twelve

MAGUIRE *wanders upstage left to lean, head bowed, against the back wall. As if he would vanish into the wall, immobile, he holds there, briefly.*

MAGUIRE *moves, slowly stumbles rather than walks towards the upstage right area, clinging to the back wall.*

Sound-track: Lili Marlene, *Dietrich version, the recording to suggest the uncertain radio in the farmhouse back of the hills.*

Upstage right, MAGUIRE *halts. Turns his attention to the downstage area, vacant attention, wanders downstage. Is drawn to the tabernacle, the gleaming door of the tabernacle. Takes out a tattered handkerchief and polishes the door. Catches his reflection in the door. Studies it — brokenly. Views his face in the door/mirror — as if he has never seen that face before.*
   MAGUIRE *breaks from the spectacle. Moves downstage, wiping his mouth with the handkerchief. Halts. Stares into the audience in desolation. Tries to say something. Fails. Moves stage-left to the kitchen-area. Gathers the loaded bag-apron and places it in the drawer. And secures the drawer in its accustomed position, sliding it slowly to. Shutting that door. His big hands against the face of the drawer, his big hands breathing no exit.*

Scene Thirteen

Two centres of simultaneous action.

(1)

MAGUIRE, *buoyant, races to the gate and bellows his (for the moment)
delight in being, in sitting on a wooden gate. Over the progress of
the* AGNES/MALONE *action (see below), he will produce a sling and
fire imaginary missiles at the sky, lie on his back on the top bar of the
gate and become the fish in the sunlit pool, straddle the gate and ride
flat out for the winning-post – and win, and, finally, flatten himself
upside down on the upstage side of the gate, face on view through the
lower bars, legs a V sprouting from the top.*

(2)

As MAGUIRE *takes to the gate,* MALONE *comes on, idles centre-stage,
boot scraping mud off his spade. Enter three* YOUNG WOMEN, AGNES
the dominant, AGNES *seductive and with basket. The three* YOUNG
WOMEN *whirl about the space, laughing, teasing* MALONE *without
restraint.*

*The basket contains a 'rope' made of four black nylons. Availing of it,
the supporting* YOUNG WOMEN *fashion a shoulder-high fence across
which* AGNES, *stage-left, ogles* MALONE, *stage-centre.*

MALONE	Christ, Agnes –
AGNES	How far's it to harvest?
MALONE	Harvest? Christ, Agnes –
AGNES	I know, I know, I know the know –

AGNES *throws a leg across the rope, rides it provocatively.*

AGNES	Play your ace –
YOUNG WOMEN	Jump . . . Jump . . . Jump . . .
AGNES	Jump –
MALONE	Ah Jaysus Agnes –
AGNES	You're soft –
YOUNG WOMEN	Soft . . . Soft . . . Soft . . .

AGNES *clears the rope. She and* THE YOUNG WOMEN *cavort about the* space, and the rope is given a new position, down-stage, waist-high, and on a cross-stage line.

AGNES is downstage of the rope. She puts down her basket. Looks at MALONE. Moistens her finger, plays it along the bobbling rope, teasily. She lifts the rope over her head, slides it down her back, sits on it, facing MALONE, swaying cheekily . . .

AGNES	Oh the men, oh the men –
YOUNG WOMEN	Oh the men, oh the men –
MALONE	She's a flamer!
AGNES	You needn't fear or fret, you needn't –
YOUNG WOMEN	Oh the men, oh the men –
AGNES	You needn't fear or fret, you needn't –
YOUNG WOMEN	Boys oh boys, boys oh boys –

AGNES, with basket, takes off again, helter-skelter. MALONE, growing excited, puts his spade-handle under the rope and THE YOUNG WOMEN assist in forming a makeshift maypole – around which they spin. MALONE is going giddy at the thoughts of daring.

MALONE	Flat in a furrow, flat in a furrow –
YOUNG WOMEN	Suck, suck-suck-suck . . . . Sooky suck-suck-suck . . .
MALONE	Over on her back!

The maypole dissolves. THE YOUNG WOMEN gambol, race upstage of the gate, return to position themselves stage-left, the rope now a little above ankle level. AGNES is poised stage-left of the rope.

MALONE, in a rush of blood, has meanwhile thrown off his coat, and is slamming the ground belligerently with the flat of his spade.

AGNES has a problem. What to do with her basket? She fires it at MALONE. MALONE drops his spade, catches the basket, gathers the spade, drops the basket, gathers the basket, shuffles in trepidation.

AGNES, uncontainable hoyden, tests the rope for resilience . . . . We hear a buzzing sound . . . . Bees? Wasps? AGNES jumps in fright, lifts her skirts, delightedly slaps her legs, knees, glowing thighs . . .

MALONE *gapes.*

The crisis passes. AGNES *resumes her frolic with the rope, pulls it playfully up to crotch-level . . .* MALONE *trembles . . .*

MALONE	Aisy, Agnes, aisy now –
YOUNG WOMEN	Aisy now, aisy now –
AGNES	Flat in a fur' for the fun of the sun . . . . Women and men for the fun of the sun . . .
MALONE	Aisy, Agnes, aisy –
AGNES	Aisy, Agnes, aisy now –
MALONE	No, Agnes, ah Christ Agnes no –

AGNES *swoops. She jumps the rope –* MALONE *drops his spade and the basket. Next* AGNES *grabs his cap and dons it and spins tauntingly about him.*

AGNES	Play your ace –
MALONE	Aisy, Agnes –
AGNES	Play your ace, play your ace –
MALONE	Ah Christ Agnes –
AGNES	Jump, jump –
YOUNG WOMEN	Flat in a fur' . . . flat in a fur' . . . flat in a fur' . . .

MALONE, *moving stage-left, flees from* AGNES *but only into the obstacle of the rope.* THE YOUNG WOMEN, *manipulating it, sweep him stage-centre and into* AGNES' *waiting arms.* THE YOUNG WOMEN *bind the pair, and exit echoing snatches from the preceding dialogue.*

AGNES *possesses* MALONE – *almost. The two struggle on the ground.* AGNES *is intent on removing his britches – and comes close to success.*

AGNES	Jump, jump –
MALONE	Mother mercy – no –
AGNES	Jump, jump –
MALONE	Mother – *Mother* –

MALONE *manages to extricate himself, palpitating fright, gathers coat and basket, and rushes off, upstage left.* AGNES *watches him depart.*

AGNES	Oh, you're soft . . . . Saint . . . . Saint . . . . Praties

and turnips, worms and frogs . . . *Matt Talbot* –

*AGNES gets up. Relaxed. She collects the rope and arranges it about
her waist. She steadies MALONE's cap on her head.*

AGNES Oh the men . . . . Oh the men . . .

She collects MALONE's spade. She studies it, her mood darkens.

AGNES Oh the men's the boys –

*She exits downstage right, dragging the spade, clatter of the spade a
harsh undertow to the rasp of her final comment.*

*MAGUIRE has been watching the climax of the AGNES/MALONE action
from his upside-down position on the gate. He holds there. He clowns,
jigging first one foot, then the other.*

*PACKY enters upstage right, a rusty tin can in his possession. He
dances slowly along a diagonal which takes him to a position
downstage left and close to THE MOTHER. He halts. He slowly lifts his
right foot, regards it.*

*As that foot rises, MAGUIRE moves from his upside-down position on
the gate, alters it to hanging, right side up, on the downstage side. He
remains suspended there, briefly.*

PACKY exits downstage left.

We hear, off, the vicious clatter of the collection-boxes.

MAGUIRE frees himself from the gate, exits upstage left, at speed.

Scene Fourteen

*The din of the collection-boxes being rattled against each other brings
AGNES on as MAGUIRE exits. AGNES, in distress, enters upstage left,*

running; she crosses the space, upstage of the gate, to exit upstage right. She re-enters downstage right and crosses to exit downstage left. Evidently cornered, she re-enters upstage left, runs downstage, halts, and howls her anguish. MARY ANNE *comes on downstage right, flourishing a collection-box as weapon and barrier.* MAGUIRE, MALONE, PACKY *and* THE SCHOOL-GIRL *arrive. All similarly armed.*

AGNES *is immobilized, mid-space. The pursuers threaten her with the din of collection-box against collection-box.* AGNES *makes a break for it –* PACKY *drives her back.* MALONE *advances, forces a collection-box on her. She accepts it – momentarily, drops it, throws it down, rather.* MAGUIRE, *broad as a bishop, puts down his box, advances on the rebel, and forces her to accept the box allocated. She complies.*

Pause. All watch to observe the extent of AGNES' *compliance. She submits, makes the opening move – stiffly raises the box towards her face – in the 'robotic dance' about to commence.*

AGNES' *surrender cues the others. All the players now move robotically about the space, their limbs – and the boxes – delivered to automation rhythms. This dance is brief, and finds climax as they stop, and face front, for a 'photo flash'.*

The 'photo flash' and accompanying sound-cue – a reverberating gong – introduces the next phase. The players slide to the ground, lie there, the boxes – however – held upright, like trees, like headstones. And the boxes sway in a lonesome breeze.

THE PRIEST *enters upstage left, takes in the spectacle. He moves towards* THE MOTHER, *and – in the lee of* THE MOTHER *– collects a handful of clay, and wanders among the sleepers blessing them with the clay. The fall of clay on each figure stills the swaying of the tree/ headstone.*

THE PRIEST'S *progress leaves him downstage right. There he collects a rattle and sounds it to rouse the sleepers.*

The sleepers rise and exit, performing various gestural scores which – echoing the robotic dance – utilize the boxes. Each player has a line which is voiced over and over.

61

MAGUIRE	Throw another sod on that fire.
AGNES	Watch him.
SCHOOL-GIRL	We ought to be finished by the morrow.
MALONE	I see you're breaking your two-year-old.
PACKY	The ace – the last game for me.
MARY ANNE	Play quick, Magure.

One player – MARY ANNE – fails to join the general exit. Locked in a phrase of her robotic dance, she remains mid-space, stranded.

THE PRIEST rescues her. He moves in, frees her, takes possession of the box, and exits with her, upstage right.

Scene Fifteen

THE SCHOOL-GIRL on – with school-bag – and a basin of oats for the hens, making chooky-chook-chook *noises as she scatters the oats. Gives the audience their share.*

SCHOOL-GIRL Oh to be wise . . .

She goes to the kitchen-area, takes from her shoulders the cardigan she's wearing, drapes it about THE MOTHER's shoulders, whispers to THE MOTHER, runs upstage, returns to THE MOTHER – gives a kiss to THE MOTHER. Upstage again now, and she races for the gate. Takes off her beret and hangs it on the left gate-post. Settles herself upstage side of the gate, peers through the bars, impish.

SCHOOL-GIRL Oh to be wise . . .

She's away again, downstage to the tabernacle: she genuflects to it – scarcely breaking stride, and arrives downstage centre. She's going to say something. She changes her mind. She moistens the tip of each index finger, gravely anoints her closed eyelids, lets her hands fall away, opens her eyes.

She sits now beside the basin. Empties her school-bag of its books.

Carefully she makes a pyramid of the books on the flat of the upturned basin, counting in Irish – 'doing her lesson' – the while.

As she starts building the pyramid, MAGUIRE *enters upstage left, rattling coins. He halts, focusses on* THE SCHOOL-GIRL, *and watches her silently from his upstage position. In the same breath,* MARY ANNE *has come on downstage left. She, in turn, focusses on* THE SCHOOL-GIRL. *Eyes on* THE SCHOOL-GIRL. *She drifts to* THE MOTHER, *and, arms about* THE MOTHER, *head resting on* THE MOTHER'*s downstage shoulder, watches, watches . . .*

The pyramid of books either collapses or is collapsed. And THE SCHOOL-GIRL *becomes a barking terrier, picks up her school-bag, and runs off upstage right, working a reprise of her counting-in-Irish verbal score.*

Scene Sixteen

MAGUIRE *advances downstage, halts stage right of* THE MOTHER. *He's rattling coins, glancing at intervals into the cup of his joined hands.* MARY ANNE *is by* THE MOTHER, *as indicated above.* MAGUIRE *gives up on the coins. The atmosphere is comfortless.*

MAGUIRE	What was I doing?
MARY ANNE	Where was I looking?
MAGUIRE	Young women and men –
MARY ANNE	Men and women – I might have joined them –
MAGUIRE	I remember a night we walked through the moon –
MARY ANNE	A moon o' Donaghmoyne –
MAGUIRE	The four of us –
MARY ANNE	Seekin' adventure –
MAGUIRE	It was mid-summer –
MARY ANNE	Summer –

MAGUIRE *resumes rattling the coins – but mime, this time, soundless. He hums morosely. And* MALONE, *drink taken and exhibiting that belligerence, comes on, upstage right, driving* PACKY *before him with the aid of an ash-plant.* PACKY *is cradling an ass-collar. Framed in the collar is a turnip-head (carved à la Hallowe'en), the head impaled on a short stick. The effect should be of a Voodoo-child, ambiguous, mocking.*

The entrance of the pair is raucous.

> MALONE   Maguire . . . Maguire . . . Maguire, you're wrong
> . . . . You're wrong about that thing I was telling
> you . . . . Poor Paddy Maguire . . . . The bridge is
> too narrow . . . the bridge is too narrow,
> Maguire . . .

MARY ANNE'S *response to the incursion is to pick up a boot downstage right and commence cleaning it, obsessively, with a corner of her apron.*

PACKY, *orchestrated by* MALONE, *is circling* MAGUIRE, *holding up the turnip-child, baiting* MAGUIRE *with the picture. And* MALONE *jeers –*

> MALONE   And thirty-five could take the sparrow's bow!

MAGUIRE *agrees to view this dubious offering, perhaps even make an offering in response – there's a mug attached to the collar, evidently a receptacle for coins. As* MAGUIRE *looks at the turnip-child,* PACKY – *manipulating the stick – slowly turns the head to meet* MAGUIRE'S *look. Pause . . .* MAGUIRE *drops his coins in the mug.* MALONE *crows triumph –*

> MALONE   And you'll have all the luck . . . . You'll have all
> the luck!

Bruised , MAGUIRE *wanders to an upstage right position, again seeks shelter against the back wall – as* MALONE *and* PACKY *sweep on in search of fresh victims.* MARY ANNE *is an obvious mark.* MALONE *loosing drover-cries, the pair descend on her. She doesn't wait to present a target – but, relinquishing her makeshift chore (the boot-cleaning), exits at speed, upstage left,* MALONE *and* PACKY *in vociferous pursuit.*

Scene Seventeen

Enter two YOUNG WOMEN *wearing black head-scarves and black aprons. They march. One carries a towel. The first briskly removes the cardigan from* THE MOTHER, *takes the bucket (downstage left), and sloshes water over the 'corpse'. The second – same brisk idiom – dries off* THE MOTHER. *Then, together, they drape a white sheet over* THE MOTHER, *and look around for –* MAGUIRE. *They spot him upstage left, sheltering by the wall. Resolutely, they march to that point, and commandeer him. He resists, shouting in Irish –*

MAGUIRE   Ná bac léi . . . Ná bac léi . . .

Nevertheless, they drag him to THE MOTHER, *drag him backwards across the space and position him beside the sheeted corpse.*

And the two YOUNG WOMEN *exit, in lockstep.*

Scene Eighteen

MAGUIRE *standing with his back to the sheeted* MOTHER. *He stretches out a hand. Touches the sheet. A spasm of fright through him. He rushes away from* THE MOTHER *and into a fit of pegging stones at the back wall, dodging their ricochet.*

That passes. Centre-stage, he takes off his cap. Blesses himself. Moves again towards THE MOTHER. *He takes the sheet and drags it away so that the face is exposed. Again he moves back, pauses centre-stage, flings his cap over the gate and away.*

He returns to THE MOTHER. *He must kiss the corpse. He circles. He moves in. He wavers. He closes. Crying like an animal, he kisses* THE MOTHER.

Again he breaks away. Rushes to the gate. Whistles for his dog. There's a surge of animal noises, and four (or more) of the players come on, upstage right and left, in animal guise. They gather upstage of the gate, battering at its bars, and the animal sounds rise to a din.

MAGUIRE – *a bucket in his clutches – stumbles towards the gate, opens the gate. The animals pour through, knocking him over, rushing over him and past him to exit variously.*

Scene Nineteen

MAGUIRE – *gathering the bucket, holding it close – scrambles upstage, humps down by the right gate-post.*

> MAGUIRE Dragged . . . . Dragged . . . . Dragged home a drunken man on a winter's night . . . . No man . . . . Helped a poor woman whose cow died on her . . . . No man . . . . Heard the young people playing on the railway stile, wished them happiness . . . . No man . . . . No man, begrudged no man his share . . . . The spade, the spade, Joe, don't forget – . . . Eileen . . . Eileen . . . Eileen. Eileen, Eileen, Eileen – who was Eileen? She was a daisy . . . . Joe, don't forget to hide the spade . . . . The fields is white . . . . Jesus, Mary, and Joseph, pray for us now and at the hour . . . Hail Holy Queen, Mother o' Mercy . . .

Scene Twenty

THE PRIEST, MARY ANNE, AGNES, THE SCHOOL-GIRL, *and* PACKY, *enter from various points.* THE PRIEST *carries his missal,* THE SCHOOL-GIRL *a lighted candle.* MALONE *brings* MAGUIRE's *overcoat and spade. He spreads the overcoat centre-stage and rests the spade on it.*

AGNES *has brought a green-leaved branch: she drops it on the overcoat.* PACKY *has brought his dented tin can: that also goes on to the overcoat. And* MARY ANNE – *in possession of* MAGUIRE's *cap – throws that on to the pile.*

THE PRIEST *rouses* MAGUIRE *by the gate-post. The two shake hands.* THE PRIEST *indicates the overcoat, the pile of objects.* MAGUIRE *goes to that point. To choose. He takes the overcoat. Puts it half-on, and moves downstage right.*

MALONE, MARY ANNE, AGNES, *and* PACKY, *recover spade, cap, branch, and tin can, respectively.*

THE PRIEST, *by the gate, is poised to lead the departure procession.*

MAGUIRE *moves centre-stage.* MALONE *shuffles forward, shakes* MAGUIRE's *hand, whispers briefly, goes upstage to wait behind* THE PRIEST. PACKY – *his tin can held like an offering – goes to* MAGUIRE. MAGUIRE *looks away.* PACKY *joins the line forming upstage.* AGNES *advances, holding her branch. She and* MAGUIRE *look at each other.* MAGUIRE *touches a leaf of the branch.* AGNES *joins the upstage line.* MARY ANNE *goes to* MAGUIRE, MARY ANNE *kneading his cap, bleakly. She doesn't look at* MAGUIRE. *His look for her is sidelong, constrained.* MARY ANNE *joins the upstage line.*

THE PRIEST *leads the procession through the gate, and off, upstage left.* THE SCHOOL-GIRL, *with lighted candle, is left. She moves quickly to close the gate, stubbing the candle in the same motion, and half-running off to catch up with the others. Close to the exit-point, she stops – as if remembering – and gives a brief backward glance to* MAGUIRE. *Then she exits freely.*

Scene Twenty-One

MAGUIRE *alone in weakening light. He moves about the space with the awkward grace of an animal nosing about for a clean place to die. His foot paws the ground searchingly – here, there, elsewhere. Soon enough he's satisfied – or he abandons the search. He lies down, gives himself to the ground.* MAGUIRE *is still.*

Finis

DIRECTOR'S NOTE

The production history of *The Great Hunger* is one of inspirations and transformations that began in the Spring of 1983 with the meeting of a writer, a director, and a player. These three became the nucleus of a theatre group that has since collaborated over five years on five productions, including a re-working of *The Great Hunger* in 1986. The script published here is the latest version of the play. It contains not only the best features of the original production, but many innovations and insights achieved through working on *The Bearded Lady* (1984), *Rise Up Lovely Sweeney* (1985) and *Dance For Your Daddy* (1987). *The Great Hunger* thus represents the beginning and the continuation of a work that is far from over. It is an initial revelation of Tom Mac Intyre's unique theatrical vision, and a compendium of many aspects of that vision subsequently revealed more fully in the other plays.

The realization of any artistic vision is a tortuous process. In the performing arts it is especially so, as the performers themselves have first to see that vision clearly , then assimilate it and make it their own. Only by bringing something into the light of consciousness can we begin to see what it is. To effect this we first go down into the dark unconscious to fetch it up. Tom Mac Intyre is a sure guide. We begin to look about and point out features along the way that the guide himself may not have noticed. He in turn is able to relate our observations to what he knows lies ahead. Sometimes the leader becomes the led, and he trusts to those around him. Eventually he brings the travellers back to the starting point, but now they know the place for the first time, transformed by their journey. Now they have the power to transform others in the alchemy of theatre.

In practical terms the steps of the journey were marked by the writing of an initial draft script which was passed between writer, director and player, until a first rehearsal script was composed. Then, in rehearsals with the company, that script developed into a performance script. In the case of *The Great Hunger* this grew into a second performance script.

The transformations were both major and minor, affecting all aspects of the play. So a green baize table in the draft script became a golden tabernacle in the rehearsal script, which in turn became a locked door and a glittery mirror in performance. A bifurcated manifestation of Maguire and Maguire Poet was reduced to pure Patrick Maguire, hanging upside down on a wooden gate. A spectral youth on the fringes of the Hiefer Romp took flesh and blood as the wandering Packy, weaving his way in and out of Maguire's days and nights, a holy fool holding the world in a rusty can. A Sacrament of Clay was suppressed and re-emerged as a dream of stiffened limbs and swaying headstones, where the 'men and wimen' go down into the ground, to be raised again by the priest's Lenten rattle.

The workplace is the shifting floor of the imagination. In every theatre that we have played, we have adapted and re-shaped our play. Edinburgh, Annaghmakerrig, Paris, Moscow, Manhattan, each setting has inspired and transformed the work because the work is alive. This published script is a description of that life, not a definition. Like all such descriptions it must animate and be animated, inspire and transform in turn, if it is to live again as theatre.

Patrick Mason
Abbey Theatre, Dublin

The Great Hunger: A Reading

The Great Hunger: A Reading

"Where the potato-gatherers like mechanised scarecrows move
Along the side-fall of the hill – Maguire and his men.
If we watch them an hour is there anything we can prove
Of life as it is broken-backed over the Book
Of Death?"

Patrick Kavanagh's long poem *The Great Hunger*, first published
in full by the Cuala Press, Dublin, in 1942, attracted immediate
attention, not all of it complimentary. It has since been recog-
nized as a major contribution to the Irish poetic canon and has
been much anthologized. In his essay on Kavanagh in *Preoccupa-
tions*, Seamus Heaney says, 'It is the nearest Kavanagh ever gets
to a grand style', while Michael O'Loughlin has argued that in
being 'true to experience rather than true to tradition [it made] a
profound break with what had been the dominant tone in Irish
literature'. Paul Durcan, however, maintains that *Lough Derg*,
written in 1942 but not published until after Kavanagh's death, is
a greater poem, being 'a microcosm of all aspects of de Valera's
Ireland, whereas *The Great Hunger* is restricted to one aspect'.

Kavanagh's own relationship with the poem was at best
ambiguous. He disparages it in the Author's Note to his *Collected
Poems* (1964), and in his short, cranky *Self-Portrait* (1964), where
he admits there are 'some queer and terrible things' in it, but
states that 'it lacks the nobility and repose of poetry'.

The Great Hunger is a poem about stagnation, enervation and
the slow, painful death of any hope of joy or fulfillment in the life
of its central character, Patrick Maguire. To Seamus Heaney, 'It is
not about growing up and away but about growing down and in.
Its symbol is the potato rather than the potato blossom.' It is also
a poem about a peasant, and poems about peasants are very rare
indeed. At least real poems about real peasants are rare. There are
too many of the other kind: inauthentic, sentimental posturing
by those for whom toil on the land is some kind of therapeutic
luxury, not the grim, soul-destroying necessity of daily
existence.

The peasant has always been a marginal figure in European literature, either idealized as a Rousseauesque natural man or dismissed as a near animal. After the poems of John Clare, in the early nineteenth century, peasants scarcely figure again in English literature. Even Hardy, whose novels have a predominantly rural setting, does not deal with them, the peasantry as a class having by then virtually disappeared in England. Elsewhere the major realist novelilsts pay them scant attention. Balzac made no real attempt to portray them in his *Comédie humaine*. Zola tried to do them justice in *The Earth* (1887), but he too confessed to a strong dislike of the peasantry, believing their lives were governed by 'simplicity and ferocity, greed and conservatism'. His naturalism was acquired, put together from observation and extensive note-taking, not truly felt.

In Russia – in many ways the closest parallel to Ireland – the peasant was frequently seen by writers and intellectuals as a mystical repository of the soul of Mother Russia. Yeats and others tried to foist a somewhat similar role upon the Irish peasant. Kavanagh feared that his own early work, the *Ploughman* poems (1936) and *The Green Fool* (1938), fell into this trap, contributing to the myth of the noble peasant content on his dungheap, and for the rest of his life he fought vigorously against it. But at his harshest he was still a poet of deep feeling who remained true to his vision even when it led him into difficult and uncomfortable areas. Any adaptation of his work needs to combine those qualities of truth telling and risk taking.

Tom Mac Intyre's adaptation of *The Great Hunger* was first staged in the Peacock Theatre, Dublin, on 9 May 1983, and revived there in July 1986 prior to its presentation at the Edinburgh Festival, where it gained massive critical acclaim and won a Fringe First Award. In Ireland it has subsequently been toured to Belfast, Waterford and Annaghmakerrig, Co. Monaghan, where it was presented in August 1986. Abroad, it has been staged in London and Paris – where it was particularly well received – in 1987. In February 1988 it went to Leningrad and Moscow, where it played in the famous Moscow Arts Theatre. The controversy aroused by that tour was at times reminiscent of the Abbey's 1912 tour to the United States with Synge's *The Playboy of the Western World*. In March 1988 *The Great Hunger* was itself taken to the USA, playing

74

in Philadelphia and New York to mixed and frequently turbulent responses.

Adaptation is a tricky business. The adaptor is faced with the problem of translating something designed for one medium into another, remaining true to the spirit of the original while satisfying the artistic demands of the new form. Few novels have transferred successfully to the stage. A poem, albeit a long one with a strong narrative line and recognizable, clearly defined characters, presents a greater challenge. Tom Mac Intyre's response to this problem is to dispense with the words and narrative structure, going straight to the heart of the poem to extract the essential images which sustain it. These he presents on stage in a series of expressionistic scenes. His adaptation's intrinsic theatricality is rooted in image and movement rather than in speech.

The first production in 1983 was an exciting experience not least for the reactions, often puzzled, sometimes hostile, which it provoked. There was much in it which the audience found striking, gripping and spellbinding, but there was much else that seemed difficult, arbitrary, even incomprehensible to them. But it provoked a reaction, an engagement with what was happening on stage, which is the true function of theatre. After each of the early performances Tom Mac Intyre and Patrick Mason (the director) came on stage to discuss and debate the play with the audience. This proved an interesting and fruitful exercise, at times even an exciting one, as members of the audience forcefully expressed their dislike and discomfort at elements of the play. As the discussions progressed, however, those who felt they had not understood what was going on were forced to admit that they had in fact taken something from it, usually more than they were at first willing to recognize.

Audience responses have tended to follow a similar pattern wherever *The Great Hunger* has been performed: initial bafflement and hostility giving way to gradual approval as the audience becomes more attuned to the form of the play. An audience anticipating a reverential treatment of a 'national classic' will have its expectations confounded. It would have been easy at this remove to pander to that expectation and bathe the audience in a comfortable glow of nostalgia, a feeling of 'Wasn't it awful then, but aren't we grand now!', as with P. J. O'Connor's 1967 adaptation of *Tarry Flynn*, re-staged at the

Abbey in 1984. With such an approach the audience, safely cocooned by the familiar form, becomes like the observers of peasant life in Section XIII of the poem; they 'stop their cars to gape over the green bank . . . touch the root of the grass and feel renewed / When they grasp the steering wheel again'. A performance of *The Great Hunger* allows no such sense of complacency to develop in its audience.

As a believer in Godard's dictum, 'a story should have a beginning, a middle and an end, but not necessarily in that order', Tom Mac Intyre has long sought a form of theatrical expression that would get away from the hidebound conventions of the well-made play; something to stir the audience and exercise a powerful and, if possible, unsettling effect on it, rather than an undemanding evening's 'entertainment' (what Peter Brook has called 'deadly theatre'). This type of non-linear, non-discursive approach is more a feature of modern cinema than of modern theatre. It is to be found especially in the work of imagistic film-makers such as Buñuel, in whose films the fantastic and mundane co-exist and whose work often incorporates elements of surrealism; Cocteau, who used dreamscapes and poetic imagery to superb effect in films such as *Orphée*; and Fellini, who frequently intermingles elements of dream and reality. Many of the characters in *The Great Hunger* might well be seen as Felliniesque grotesques, bringing to mind such figures as the sex-starved uncle in *Amacord*, while the sexual taunting of the men by Agnes and the other young girls would not be out of place in a Fellini film. Another strand of modern cinema which has influenced the staging of *The Great Hunger* is the visionary films of Pasolini, Herzog and especially Tarkovsky, whose use of religious imagery in such films as *Mirror* and *Stalker* is reflected in some of the stark religious images of the play. As a one-time film critic for *The Standard*, Kavanagh might have appreciated the impact film has had on this adaptation of his work.

The Great Hunger is a play in which the images presented on stage carry all the weight. It appeals more to the heart than to the mind, to feelings rather than intellect. To appreciate it fully as a piece of theatre, we must allow the images to work their magic on us. One of the most effective moments, for example, is when Maguire and one of his men, Malone, stand leaning over the five bar gate smoking cigarettes and staring silently at the audience

(Scene Four). They remain like that for a short time, then the lights go down and in the darkness only the glow of the two cigarettes can be seen on stage. Such expression of silent desperation, the failure of communication and the sense of fellow feeling between characters, can only be conveyed fully in theatre. There are many such moments in *The Great Hunger*. In another scene (Scene Three) Maguire tries to blow life into a dying fire with the bellows, blowing more and more vigorously until the action becomes a mime of frantic masturbation, reflecting those passages in the poem where Maguire attempts to relieve his sexual frustration by 'bringing the vague / Women of his mind to lust nearness', passages which led Brendan Behan to dub Kavanagh 'the Monaghan wanker'!

Such scenes are not the only notable feature of the play. The 'dialogue', if such a term can be used to describe the overlapping, often repetitive, sometimes distorted speech patterns of the characters, is poetic, heightened, rhythmical, imagistic and redolent of rural Ireland, whether in the form of rich idiomatic phrases peppered throughout the play, like the wonderfully expressive 'Oh the men's the boys' – which gave such difficulties to the Russian translators, being rendered as 'men used to be children' – , or in the almost incantatory use of such phrases as 'Patrick Maguire went home and made cocoa', which recurs like a despairing refrain as all of Maguire's hopes and dreams fade and die inexorably.

Despite its daring formal devices and theatrical inventiveness, *The Great Hunger* is as rooted in the realities of rural Ireland as are John B. Keane's *The Field* and Eugene McCabe's *King of the Castle* (from the same Monaghan background), two of the finest Irish plays of the last twenty years. It conveys a deep feeling for life as it is lived in the Cavan-Monaghan area (the Kavanagh country) where small farms predominate and their owners attempt to squeeze a meagre living from the boggy, lake-covered lowlands, or from the 'stony grey soil' of the ridges and drumlins.

The detail in both set and costume is tellingly accurate, as in Maguire's bag-apron, once a ubiquitous item in the working apparel of Irish farmers. Rooted in quotidian reality, the play remains true to the spirit of the poem, conveying both its earthiness and its essentially tragic vision of the peasant life. We see the sensitive, trapped figure of Patrick Maguire, the archetypal peasant, being drained of life and hope by the unrelenting toil he must endure simply to survive. Surrounded by Nature, he denies its strongest urge, his own sexuality, at the behest of church and mother (Mother Church!), the twin totems which overshadow his life and to which he, in his alternate roles as son and supplicant, constantly pays obeisance.

But the set manages to convey more than mere surface reality elements of it also have a symbolic function. The iconic figure of the mother dominates the stage, occupying an ambiguous position as both giver and sapper of life. The unquestioned authority of the Church is represented by the mute tabernacle, more than by the all-too-worldly figure of the priest.

Some scenes seek to transcend the everyday world, for example the procession (Scene Five) reaches back beyond Christianity to more primitive, pagan forms of religion which were an active ingredient in Irish folk tradition until the mid-nineteenth century, and vestiges of which still survive. The survival of pre-Christian myths and beliefs is also a theme in Mac Intyre's later *Rise Up Lovely Sweeney*. A similar sense of elemental forces in the Irish psyche is found in the poetry of Nuala Ní Dhomhnaill, with its motifs of the *lios*, the *cailleach* and the *spéirbhean*.

It is hard to imagine who other than Tom Mac Intyre might have staged *The Great Hunger*. His career has been diverse, at times wayward, but the range of forms he has explored has equipped him for the task he set himself. Beginning with the sub-Mylesian novel, *The Charollais* (1969), and the relatively conventional short stories of his first collection, *Dance the Dance* (1970), he has moved restlessly from reportage in *Through the Bridewell Gate* (1971) to poetry and translation, *Blood Relations* (1972) and *I Bailed Out at Ardee* (1987). Of all these literary activities it is his lively, playful and earthy translations of seventeenth- and eighteenth-century Gaelic poetry, principally in *Blood Relations* (contrast his version of 'The Yellow Bittern' with Thomas MacDonagh's better known but staid and academic rendering), and the dense, imagistic, elliptical stories in his second collection *The Harper's Turn* (1982), written when working on his adaptation of the poem, which have most bearing on the form of his play.

Theatre has been a liberation for him. Here he found a medium which could encompass the range of his talents and interests,

78

accommodating both the verbal and the visual, admitting the exhilarating possibilities of experiment while remaining rooted in concrete reality. From *Eye-Winker Tom-Tinker* (1972) he began to develop his theatrical concerns through a series of plays staged mostly in the Peacock Theatre, working his way slowly towards the theatrical forms he employs today. The time he spent in Paris in 1978-79, working with an American dance company, the Calck Hook Dance Theatre of New York, was crucial in this regard. With them he developed *Doobally – Back Way* (staged in Dublin in 1979), a play which is in many ways the immediate precursor of *The Great Hunger*.

Tom Mac Intyre is, of course, a Cavanman, and they're a breed unto themselves. The wily Cavanman is a mythic figure in Irish folklore, on a par with the cute Kerryman and the subject of almost as many jokes and stories. Mac Intyre ascribes this to the frontier mentality (in an article written for Aer Lingus's *Cara* magazine). Cavan has always been borderland. The drumlin belt marks the southernmost extent of glacial activity in Ireland during the last Ice Age. It is a natural as well as a mental boundary. In the Early Historic period it was the southern frontier of the kingdom of *Ulaid*. Parts of the linear earthwork known as 'The Black Pig's Dyke' once ran across Cavan. The route of the *Táin* was through this hilly land. In medieval times it was swordland, subject of continual dispute as the local Gaelic families, the O'Reillys and the O'Rourkes of Breiffne, fought for possession with the Anglo-Norman settlers, from the Lordship of Meath to the south and the Earldom of Ulster to the north. For the Elizabethans it was the frontier between Gaelic Ulster and the lands controlled by government forces. Later still it became the dividing-line between Plantation Ulster and the areas still occupied by the native Irish. Today it is 'border country' with all that that implies of tension, uncertainty and division. Is it any wonder that its most famous symbol is the Iron Age figure known as the Corleck Head, which being three-faced looks three ways at once. This land is in Mac Intyre's blood. He's enough of a Cavanman to be adept at the sidestep. He's not likely to be caught by such questions as 'What does it mean?'

Cavan is also an area where mummers and the tradition of mumming plays is still a living force, a fact we should not forget when grappling with the form of Mac Intyre's theatre. However,

Mac Intyre didn't develop and doesn't work in a vacuum up there in the drumlins of Cavan. His work belongs to an international context and tradition called the Theatre of the Image. This line of theatrical endeavour developed out of the search for new forms in the early twentieth century. Among the most important was the Russian director and theoretician Vsevolod Meyerhold, a ceaseless experimenter who sought to define the theatrical equivalent of literary modernism. He used elements of the new Soviet art form known as 'Constructivism' in stage design, and insisted that the text and the actors should be subordinate to stage setting, inventing the pseudo-scientific term 'biomechanics' to describe this process. Working in the 1920s during the great age of Soviet cinema, the era of Eisenstein and Pudovkin, Meyerhold was very influenced by the developments in cinematic technique. So much could be done better by cinema that it was imperative for theatre to find space for itself by developing its strengths which he argued lay primarily in taking a non-naturalistic approach. Eventually he fell foul of the Stalinist drive for conformity and disappeared, presumed executed (c. 1940), in the purges.

Working in analogous areas were the British stage designer Edward Gordon Craig and the French actor-director Antonin Artaud, whose manifestoes of the early 1930s advocated reawakening the primitive power of theatre by freeing it from the constraints of formal texts and appealing directly to the unconscious mind through gesture, movement and spectacle.

The quest for new forms of theatrical expression inaugurated at that time has continued and been further developed. In recent decades the work of Jerzy Grotowski and the Polish Laboratory Theatre, and of Kazimierz Braun and the Wroclaw Contemporary Theatre Company, has been at the forefront of these movements. It has been primarily a continental phenomenon. Craig was never really appreciated in Britain and worked mostly abroad. Similarly the most experimental of contemporary British directors, Peter Brook, has found his best audiences in Europe and America.

In Ireland, despite the example of Yeats, the naturalistic mode has prevailed and experimental theatre of this type has rarely been attempted. The Wroclaw Company's two visits to the Dublin Theatre Festival, with *Birthrate* in 1981 and *Anna Livia* (based on sections of *Finnegans Wake*) in 1982, generated a lot of excitement and curiosity and contributed to the theatrical education of Irish performers and audiences by making them familiar with this form of theatre.

The greatest strength of the Theatre of the Image lies in its freshness and vitality. At its best a tremendous energy can be released, both in performers and audience. At worst it can lead to obscurity, wilfullness and self-indulgence, and all too easily become inaccessible, leaving audiences locked outside of its self-referential framework. So far, Tom Mac Intyre and his collaborators have avoided this.

Though all theatre is by definition collaborative, in *The Great Hunger* and subsequent works the degree of collaboration is greater than usual. This facet was always stressed by Mac Intyre and Mason in their post-production audience discussions. Central to the enterprise has been the core group of Mac Intyre (writer), Patrick Mason (director) and Tom Hickey (principal actor).

Hickey's outstanding performance as Patrick Maguire is central to the success of the play. Trained in the Stanislavski method in the Focus Theatre, Dublin, Hickey was already known for his diverse roles in Brecht's *Galileo*, Lanford Wilson's *Talley's Folly* and Neil Donnelly's *The Silver Dollar Boys*. With *The Great Hunger* he stretched his range beyond the naturalistic portrayal of character, using gesture, mime and facial expression to their fullest, as he was later to do in his moving performance as Joe in Alan Gilsenan's film of Beckett's *Eh Joe*. His contribution to *The Great Hunger*, followed later in 1983 by his towering performance as J. P. W. King in Tom Murphy's *The Gigli Concert*, confirmed his position as one of the leading actors of his generation.

Between them, the Mac Intyre-Mason-Hickey triumvirate have schooled a team of actors, including mime and dance artists, in the basic theatrical vocabulary needed to give effective life to their projects. Since *The Great Hunger* they have embarked on a series of productions, all in the Peacock Theatre. *The Bearded Lady* (1984) took Swift as its subject, focussing on his troubled relationships with women. This was the least successful of their efforts, and never really got to grips with its elusive subject. *Rise Up Lovely Sweeney* (1985) was derived from the early Irish saga *Buile Suibhne*, while *Dance For Your Daddy* (1987) concerned the love and tensions between fathers and daughters.

Seamus Heaney, commenting on the poetics of *The Great Hunger*, wrote, 'Kavanagh's technical achievement here is to find an Irish note that is not dependent on backward looks towards the Irish tradition.' Tom Mac Intyre's dramatization has also found a distinctive Irish note without being held in thrall to the Irish dramatic tradition. Yet at many points it acknowledges that tradition, while taking it a step, or even several steps, farther, challenging our perceptions of the 'action' and the modes chosen to express it, and obliging us to find our own way, or ways, into its world. Our response to that challenge determines the quality of what we take from the experience.

How would Patrick Kavanagh himself have reacted to this treatment of his work? By attacking and stripping down *The Great Hunger*, Tom Mac Intyre has succeeded in eliminating that 'kinetic vulgarity' its over-conscientious author later detected, and by restoring an element of comedy while retaining the essential tragedy, he has given back to it the 'true detachment' proper to a work of art. That great admirer of *Godot*, who praised Beckett's honesty in putting 'despair and futility on the stage for us to laugh at', would surely have approved.

REFERENCES AND BIBLIOGRAPHY

Artaud, Antonin. *The Theatre and its Double* (John Calder, London 1970).

Bentley, Eric (ed.). *The Theory of the Modern Stage* (Penguin Books, London 1976).

Braun, Edward (ed.). *Meyerhold on Theatre* (Methuen, London 1978).

Brook, Peter. *The Empty Space* (Penguin Books, London 1972).

Durcan, Paul. 'Foreword' to *Lough Derg*, a poem by Patrick Kavanagh (Martin Brian & O'Keefe, London 1978).

Grotowski, Jerzy. *Towards a Poor Theatre* (Methuen, London 1975).

Heaney, Seamus. 'From Monaghan to the Grand Canal: The Poetry of Patrick Kavanagh' in *Preoccupations, Selected Prose 1968-1978* (Faber & Faber, London 1980).

Kavanagh, Patrick. *Collected Poems* (Martin Brian & O'Keeffe, London 1964).

— *Self-Portrait* (Dolmen Press, Dublin 1964).

— *'Waiting for Godot'* in *Collected Pruse* (Martin Brian & O'Keefe, London 1973).

Kumiega, Jennifer. *The Theatre of Grotowski* (Methuen, London 1987).

Mac Intyre, Tom. *Blood Relations; versions of Gaelic Poems of the 17th and 18th Centuries* (New Writers Press, Dublin 1972).

— *The Harper's Turn* (Gallery Press, Dublin 1982).

— 'All The Lakes is Haunted' in *Cara* (Aer Lingus flight magazine, Nov.-Dec. 1986).

O'Loughlin, Michael. *After Kavanagh; Patrick Kavanagh and the discourse of contemporary Irish poetry* (Raven Arts Press, Dublin 1985).

Walton, J. Michael (ed.). *Craig on the Theatre* (Methuen, London 1983).